A difficult legal problem is a disaster for most people. Lawyers are expensive and not always trustworthy. Court procedures and language are difficult to understand and often frightening. The person with the legal problem (the client) is commonly denied the right to participate in his or her own dispute, except to pay and pay and pay.

In the midst of this unhappy picture there are several rays of light. One is Small Claims Court — a place where decisions are made cheaply, quickly and with the participation of the disputing parties. In this book Ralph Warner shows you how to use Small Claims Court to your best advantage. With the information given here and your own creativity and determination, there is much that you can do to liberate yourself from the oppression of lawyers, judges and our traditional court system.

"Warner's book takes you by the hand through all the potential pitfalls of trying your own case. But, before you file against someone who has done you in, Warner says you should make an honest attempt at settling the dispute. He has devoted a whole section of the book on how to wangle a settlement . . ."

— Peter Weaver
Los Angeles Times

"This is a superb book! Flawless! No small business should be without it . . ."

— Michael Phillips
The Next Whole Earth Catalogue

"Everybody's Guide to Small Claims Court *gives step-by-step advice on how to prepare your case, how to file it, and perhaps most importantly, how to collect if you win. It outlines several ways to determine if it's worth suing and also presents various methods of collecting the money if you do win."*

— Steve Fox
Associated Press

"So you sent your suit to the cleaners and it came back a bit too small for Mickey Rooney? Sue the bums. And here's your book: a straight-forward guide to the basic substantive law and procedural mechanics involved in bringing various typical small claims actions."
— Kirkus Reviews

"Warner defines some basic legal jargon and urges potential plaintiffs to evaluate whether their cases are worth the effort of bringing them to court. He outlines examples of common types of cases and suggests strategies for tackling them. Warner has put together a concise, objective guide."
— Publishers Weekly

"The book takes the potential litigant through every step of the dispute-resolution process, from deciding whether a claim exists to filing the right papers and presenting the best possible case before the judge . . . It is fast reading and, for the sense of power and potential savings in unnecessary legal fees it gives the reader, well worth the price."
— Liza Schlafly
Atlanta Journal Constitution

"You can find good counsel in attorney Ralph Warner's Everybody's Guide to Small Claims Court... *Warner's handbook can be a useful guide to everything from how to resist to how to collect."*
— Martin Levin
Associated Press

Everybody's Guide to

small claims court

by Ralph Warner

research: David W. Brown

950 Parker St., Berkeley, CA 94710

Nolo Press is committed to keeping its books up-to-date. Each new printing, whether or not it is called a new edition, has been completely revised to reflect the latest law changes. If you are using this book any considerable time after the last date listed below, be particularly careful not to rely on information without checking it.

First Edition	April 1978
Second Edition	February 1979
Second Printing	July 1979
Third Edition	March 1981
Fourth Edition	March 1982
Fifth Edition	September 1983

▲

Editors:	David Brown
	Leslie Ihara Armistead
Illustrations:	Linda Allison
Graphics:	Daniel Foley
Production:	Jackie Clark

Library of Congress Catalog No. 81-80355
ISBN: 0-917316-63-0
© Copyright 1978, 1981 & 1983 by Ralph Warner

Thank You

Nolo Press is as much family as business. Without the help of family members Trudy Ahlstrom, Toni Ihara, Keija Kimura, Linda Allison, Yolanda Gonzalez and Carol Pladsen, there would be no books such as this one.

A number of talented friends read the manuscript of this book and made helpful suggestions for improvement. With enough help, even a tarnished penny can be made to shine. Thanks to Dan Armistead, Leslie Ihara Armistead, David Brown, Peter Honigsberg, Ellen Roddy, Steve Elias, Jeanne Stott, Roderic Duncan, Linda Dyson, Delores Huajardo and Jody Anne Becker.

▼

CAUTION: Although care has been taken to ensure the accuracy of the information contained here, no one is perfect and we ask you not to make decisions based on what you read here without getting a copy of your local Small Claims Court rules and checking the information carefully. Neither Nolo Press nor the author assumes any responsibility or liability in connection with the information contained in this book or the use to which it is put.

UPDATE SERVICE & LEGAL DIRECTORY

Our books are as current as we can make them, but sometimes the laws do change between editions. You can read about any law changes which may affect this book in the **NOLO NEWS**, a 12 page newspaper which we publish quarterly.

In addition to the **Update Service**, each issue contains a directory of people-oriented lawyers and legal clinics available to answer questions, handle a complicated case or process your paperwork at a reasonable cost. Also featured are comprehensive articles about the growing self-help law movement as well as areas of the law that are sure to affect you.

To receive the next 4 issues of the **NOLO NEWS**, please send us $2.00.

Name_____

Address _____

_____

Send to: **NOLO PRESS**, 950 Parker St., Berkeley, CA 94710

Contents

Introduction

Here is a practical book on how to use Small
Claims Court. It is a tool which will help you
answer such questions as:

"How does Small Claims Court work?"

"Do I have a case worth pursuing or defending?"

"How do I prepare my case to maximum advantage?"

"What witnesses and other evidence should I
present?"

"What do I say in court?"

"Can I appeal if I lose?"

"How do I collect my judgment?"

Proper preparation of your Small Claims action
can often mean the difference between receiving a
check and writing one. This isn't to say that I can
tell you how to take a hopeless case and turn it into
a blue ribbon winner. It does mean that with the
information you will learn here and your own creativity and common sense, you will be able to develop
your position in the best possible way. It does mean
that I can show you how a case with a slight limp can
be improved and set on four good legs.

Just as important as knowing when and how to
bring your Small Claims Court action is knowing when
not to. You don't want to waste time and energy
dragging a hopeless case to court. Here we will
teach you to understand the difference between win-
ners and losers, and hopefully to keep the losers at
home.

The goal of this book is to give both people
bringing a case and those defending one all the
step-by-step information necessary to make the best
possible use of Small Claims Court. From deciding
whether you have a case, through gathering evidence,
arranging for witnesses, planning your courtroom
presentation, and collecting your money, you will
find everything you need here.

Certain arbitrary decisions have had to be
made as to order and depth of coverage. For example,
the question of whether an oral contract is valid is
discussed in Chapter 2, but not again in Chapter 16
on automobile repairs, where you may need it. So
please take the time to read, or at least skim, the
entire book before you focus on the chapters that
interest you most. You may find something on page
106 that will change what you learned on page 32. A
good way to get an overview of the entire Small
Claims process is by carefully reading the Table of
Contents. It would be worthwhile to read it through
several times before starting the text itself.

Chapter 24 is the last part of this book
designed to help you win your case and collect your
money. Chapter 25 is devoted to a different

cause--how our court system must be changed to
deliver more justice and less frustration. In many
ways this material is intensely personal in that it
reflects my own experience with our formal, lawyer-
dominated legal delivery system. It springs from my
own painful realization that neither law, nor justice, nor the resolution of disputes is what our
courts are presently about. We have instead allowed
them to become the private fiefdom of lawyers, judges
and other professionals, and it is their selfish
interests rather than the common good that are being
served.

I have included this material because I believe
that it will be of interest to all of you who have
become involved in the resolution of your own disputes in Small Claims Court. You have had the cour-
age to take responsibility for solving your own problems. Given the opportunity, you can do a great deal
more. It is past time that you are allowed to participate in your own legal system. It is past time
that you are made welcome in your own courthouses.
It is past time that all of us realize that a society
whose legal system is run by and for lawyers can't
long survive.

1.

In the Beginning

A. First Things

In this book we will be discussing Small Claims
Court in California. As Small Claims procedures are
established by state law, there are differences in
their operating rules, state-to-state. Differences
include such things as the maximum amount that you
can sue for, who can sue, and what papers must be
filed, where and when. However, the differences
between Small Claims Court in California and other
states tend to be those of detail, not substance.
The basic approaches necessary to properly prepare
and present a case are remarkably similar everywhere.
For this reason, we have been able to also produce a
50-state version of this book. So, if you are outside of California, you will want to see Everybody's
Guide to Small Claims Court (National Edition). See
the back of this book for order information.

The purpose of Small Claims Court is to hear disputes involving small amounts of money, without long delays and formal rules of evidence. Disputes are presented by the people involved and lawyers are normally prohibited.[1] The maximum amount of money that can be sued for in California is $1,500 (this is often called the "jurisdictional amount" in legal jargon). This is about average, although there is considerable variation with some states allowing Small Claims cases involving thousands of dollars, and others limiting Small Claims Court to cases worth no more than two or three hundred dollars.[2]

There are three great advantages of Small Claims Court. First, you get to prepare and present your own case without having to pay a lawyer more than your claim is worth.[3] This right to self-representation should be radically expanded to types of cases not now permitted in Small Claims Court. Unfortunately, such expansion runs counter to the self-interest of lawyers, who, like the czars of old Russia or the French nobility at the time of the Revolution, will fight to the death rather than ease the way for sensible reform.

The second great advantage to bringing a dispute to Small Claims Court is simplicity. The gobbledy-gook of complicated legal forms and language are kept to a minimum. To start your case, you need only fill out a few lines on a simple form (i.e., "Honest Al's Used Chariots owes me $500 because the 1972 Chevette they sold me in supposedly 'excellent condition' died less than a mile from the car lot"). When you get to court, you can talk to the judge without a whole lot of "res ipsa loquiturs" and "pendente lites." If you have documents, or witnesses, you may present them

_____

1 In California, a lawyer may sue in his own case and as the representative of a corporation under some circumstances (see Chapter 8).

2 The laws listing how much you can sue for, as well as the procedure in Small Claims Court, are listed in the California "Code of Civil Procedure" (C.C.P.), in Sections 116 through 117.20.

3 People who have language difficulties are entitled to help in presenting their cases. Small Claims Court clerks maintain lists of volunteer interpreters.

for what they are worth with no requirement that you comply with the thousand year's accumulation of fusty, musty procedures, habits and so-called rules of evidence of which the legal profession is so proud.

Third, and perhaps more important, Small Claims Court doesn't take long. Most disputes are heard in court within a month or two from the time the complaint is filed. The judge makes his (her) decision on the basis of what is presented in the courtroom, and normally renders a decision within a few days.

But before you decide that Small Claims Court sounds like just the place to bring your case, you will want to answer a basic question. Are the results you are likely to achieve in proportion to, or greater than, the effort you will have to expend? This must be answered individually, and the answers may be very different. It is all too easy to get so involved in a dispute that you lose sight of the fact that the time, trouble and expense of continuing are way out of balance with any likely return.

In order to profitably think about whether your case is worth the effort, you will want to understand the details of how Small Claims Court works--who can sue, where, for how much, etc. You will also want to learn a little law--are you entitled to relief, how much, and how do you compute the exact amount? Finally and most importantly comes the detail that so many people overlook to their later dismay. Assuming that you prepare and present your case brilliantly, and get a judgment for everything you request, can you collect? This seems a silly thing to overlook, doesn't it? Sad to say, however, it is often done. Plaintiffs commonly go through the entire Small Claims procedure with no chance of collecting a dime because they have sued a person with no money.

The purpose of the first dozen chapters of this book is to help you decide whether or not you have a case worth pursuing. These are not the Perry Mason sections where grand strategies are brilliantly unrolled to baffle and confound the opposition--that comes later. Here we are more concerned with what Della Street does off camera--such mundane tasks as locating the person you want to sue, suing in the right court, filling out the various forms and getting them properly served. Perhaps it will disappoint those of you with a dramatic turn of mind, but most cases are won or lost before anyone enters the courtroom.

Throughout this book we reproduce sample forms used in one or another judicial district in California. All California Small Claims forms contain about the same information although they are often laid out differently from one judicial district to the next. So, if you live in Los Angeles, don't be put off because we reproduce a San Francisco form, as the one in use in Los Angeles will be substantially similar. Blank copies of all these forms are available at your local Small Claims clerk's office. Forms in use outside of California will look somewhat different, but you will find that they are easy to understand everywhere.

B. Checklist of Things to Think Out Before Initiating or Defending Your Case

Here is a sort of preliminary checklist of
things you will want to think about at this initial
stage. As you read further we will go into each of
these areas in more detail. But let me remind you
again, if you haven't already gotten a copy of your
local Small Claims Court rules, do it now. It's
silly to come to bat with two out in the ninth and
the bases loaded and not know if you are supposed to
run to first or third.

Checklist of Questions
Needing Answers Before You
File in Small Claims Court:

1. Does the other person owe you the money, or,
put another way, "is there liability"? (See Chapter
2)

2. How many dollars is your claim for? If it
is more for than the Small Claims maximum, do you
wish to waive the excess and still use Small Claims?
(See Chapter 4)

3. Is your suit brought within the proper time
period (Statute of Limitations)? (See Chapter 5)

4. What Small Claims Court should you bring
your suit in? (See Chapter 9)

5. Whom do you sue? As you will see in many
cases, especially those involving businesses and
automobiles, this can be a little more technical and
tricky than you might have guessed. (See Chapter 8)

6. Have you made a reasonable effort to contact
the other party to offer a compromise? (See Chapter
6)

7. And again, the most important question--
assuming that you can win, is there a reasonable
chance that you can collect? (See Chapters 3 and 23)

Checklist of Questions
Needing Answers Before
Defending A Case:

1. Do you have a good defense to the claim of the plaintiff? (See Chapters 2 and 12)

2. Has the plaintiff sued for a reasonable or an excessive amount? (See Chapter 4)

3. Has the plaintiff brought his/her suit within the proper time limits (Statute of Limitations)? (See Chapter 5)

4. Has the plaintiff followed reasonably correct procedures in bringing suit and serving you with the court papers? (See Chapters 11 and 12)

5. Have you made a reasonable effort to contact the plaintiff in order to arrive at a compromise settlement? (See Chapters 6 and 12)

DEFENDANT'S NOTE: In addition to your right to defend a case, you also have the right to file your own claim (Chapters 10 and 12). You would want to do this if you believed that you suffered damage arising from the same incident or transaction that formed the basis of the plaintiff's suit against you, and that the plaintiff was responsible for your loss. Defendants' claims commonly develop out of a situation where both parties were negligent (say in a car accident) and the question to be decided is who was most at fault.

C. Legal Jargon Defined

Mercifully, there is not a great deal of technical language in use in Small Claims Courts. But there are a few terms that may be new to you and which you will have to become familiar with. Don't try to learn all of these terms now. Refer back to these definitions when you need them.

ABSTRACT OF JUDGMENT: An official document which you get from the Small Claims Court clerk's office which shows you that you have a money judgment against another person.

CALIFORNIA CIVIL CODE (C.C.) and CALIFORNIA CODE OF CIVIL PROCEDURE (C.C.P.): Books which contain some of California's substantive and procedural laws. Available at all public libraries and law libraries (which are located at the county courthouse and are open to the public).

CLAIM OF DEFENDANT: A claim by a defendant that the plaintiff owes him money. A Claim of Defendant is filed as part of the same lawsuit that the plaintiff has started.

CLAIM OF EXEMPTION: A procedure by which a "judgment debtor" can claim that under federal and/or California law certain of his money or other property is exempt from being grabbed to satisfy the debt.

CONTINUANCE: A court order that a hearing be postponed to a later date.

DEFAULT JUDGMENT: A court decision given when one person fails to show up (defaults).

DEFENDANT: The person being sued.

EQUITY: The value of a particular piece of property that you actually own. For example, if a car has a fair market value of $2,000 and you owe a bank $1,000 on it, your equity is $1,000.

GARNISH: To attach money, usually wages or commissions, for payment of a debt.

HOMESTEAD DECLARATION: A piece of paper that any homeowner can file with the County Recorder's office which protects the equity in his/her home from attachment and sale to satisfy most debts. The protection is $45,000 in equity for a family and persons who are over 65 or blind, and $30,000 for a single person.

JUDGMENT: The decision rendered by the court.

JUDGMENT CREDITOR: A person to whom money is owed under a court decision.

JUDGMENT DEBTOR: A person who owes money under a court decision.

LEVY: A legal method to seize property or money for unpaid debts. For example, a sheriff could levy on (sell) your automobile if you refused to pay a judgment.

LIEN: A legal right to an interest in the property of another for payment of a debt. To get a lien you first must get a court judgment and then take proper steps to have the court enter an "Abstract of Judgment." You can then take the Abstract to the County Recorder's office in a county where the judgment debtor has real property to establish the lien.

ORDER OF EXAMINATION: A court procedure allowing a creditor to question a debtor about the extent and location of his or her assets.

PLAINTIFF: The person who starts a lawsuit.

RECORDER (OFFICE OF THE COUNTY RECORDER): The person employed by the county to make and record documents. The County Recorder's office is usually located in the main county courthouse.

STATUTE OF LIMITATIONS: The time period in which you must file your lawsuit. It is normally figured from the date the act or omission giving rise to the lawsuit occurs and varies depending on the type of suit. See Chapter 5.

WRIT OF EXECUTION: An order by a court to the sheriff of a specific county to collect a specific amount of money due.

2.

Do You Have a Case?

Before you even start thinking about going to court--any court--you must answer a basic question. Do I have a good case?

Many mornings I have sat in Small Claims Court and watched people competently and carefully present hopeless cases. Why hopeless? Usually because the plaintiffs overlooked one of the most basic facts of litigation. Before you can collect for a loss you have suffered, you must show that the other party caused you to suffer the loss. Put into legal slang, this means that you must show that there is "liability." Obvious, you say. Perhaps it is to you, but apparently not to lots of others.

Here is what often seems to happen. People focus on their own loss--the amount of money that they are out as a result of whatever incident occurred. They think that, because they have been damaged, they must have a right of recovery against someone. But the fact that a loss has occured isn't enough to make a winning case. You must also prove that the person you are suing is legally responsible to compensate you for the loss. Often doing this is easy and obvious and sometimes it is neither.

How do you establish that another person owes you money? Or put another way, how do you establish "liability"? Normally, you must establish at least one of the following three things. There are a number of technical legal defenses to all of these approaches, but for now, let's just look at the general theories.

1. That a valid contract (written, oral or implied) has been broken by the person you are suing and that, as a result, you have suffered money damages (see A below);

2. That the intentional behavior of the person you are suing has caused you to suffer money damages (see B below);

3. That the negligent behavior of the person you are suing has caused you to suffer money damages (see B below).

Before we look at each of these theories of "liability" in detail, let me tell you the story of a case I watched recently in Small Claims Court in Berkeley, California. The plaintiff (remember, the plaintiff is the person who initiates the lawsuit), a college student, had rented a parking space in the basement garage of an apartment house owned by defendant. There was a driveway entrance door to the garage that could be shut and locked, sealing the garage from the street. However, as the tenants were unwilling to go to the trouble of opening and closing the door, it always stood open. Indeed, the door had been open night and day for years, including the six months during which plaintiff had kept her car in the garage. There was also access to the garage from inside the building which contained 15 apartments, most of them occupied by more than one person.

One night someone entered the garage, smashed a window in plaintiff's (let's call her Sue) car and stole a fancy AM-FM radio and tape deck worth $528.50. Upon discovery of the theft, Sue immediately got several witnesses to the fact that her car had been broken into. She took pictures and then called the police. After the police investigation was complete, Sue obtained a copy of their investigation report. She also got several estimates as to the cost of repairing the damage to the car window, the lowest of which was $157.00. Sue then filed suit against the building owner for $685.50.

Sue overlooked only one thing. Unfortunately for her, it was an important one. Under the circumstances the building owner wasn't liable. He never promised (orally or in writing) to keep the garage locked, had never done so, had never led Sue to believe that he would do so, and indeed could point to requests from other tenants that the garage be kept open. All the tenants were reasonably on notice that it was easy to gain access to the garage either from inside or outside the building. Put simply, the building owner was neither in violation of a contract, nor guilty of any negligent behavior in failing to lock the garage. The situation facing Sue was no different than it would have been if her car had been damaged in the street.

Now let's take this same situation, but change a few facts. Instead of a situation where the door was always open and no one ever expected it to be closed, let's now assume that the lease contract signed by the landlord and tenant stated that the tenant would be assigned a parking place in a "locked garage." Let's also assume that the garage had always been locked until the lock broke seven days before the theft occurred. Finally, let's assume that Sue and other tenants had asked the owner to fix the lock the day after it broke, but that he hadn't "gotten around to it."

In this situation, Sue should win. The landlord made certain promises to the tenant (to keep the garage locked) and then failed to keep them in a situation where he had ample opportunity to do so. The failure presumably allowed the robber access to the car.

NOTE: In both fact situations above, the total amount of damage, $685,50, was the same. But in the first, there was no right of recovery (the defendant wasn't liable), and in the second, the apartment owner's failure to keep the door locked violated defendant's lease contract. In addition, the failure of the apartment owner to fix the lock within a reasonable time constituted negligence.

A. How to Approach a Breach of Contract Case

In broad outline, a contract is any agreement between parties where one person agrees to do something for the other in exchange for something in return. The agreement may be written, oral, or implied from the circumstances (i.e., I deliver milk to your house and you pay for it).[1]

EXAMPLE 1: "I promise to give you $750 on the first of January." This is not a contract because you have promised to do nothing for me in return. I have only indicated that I will give you a gift in the future. This sort of promise is not enforceable.

EXAMPLE 2: "I promise to pay you $750 on January 1 in exchange for your promise to shine my door knob every morning before 7 o'clock." This is a valid contract. If I refuse to pay you, you can go to court and get a judgment for the $750.

---

1 Contracts that can't be performed within a year must be in writing. However, the great majority of consumer-type contracts can be performed in a year and therefore oral contracts are normally enforceable.

Perhaps the largest number of cases coming before Small Claims Court involve the breach of a contract. Often the contract that has not been honored involves a failure to pay money. Hardly a day goes by when someone isn't sued for failing to pay the phone company, the milkman, the local hospital, or even book fines to the public library. But sometimes a breach of contract suit stems, not from failure to pay a bill, but because one party has performed his/her duties under the contract badly, or not at all, and the other person has been damaged as a result. Such might be the case if an apartment owner accepted a deposit and agreed to rent an apartment to a tenant and then rented it to someone else.[2]

Damages resulting from a breach of contract are normally not difficult to prove. You must show that the contract existed (if it is written, it should be presented to the court, and if it's oral or implied from the circumstances, it should be stated). You must then testify as to the circumstances of the other person's breach of the contract and the amount of damages you have suffered. In many situations this involves no more than stating that a legitimate bill for X dollars has not been paid.

EXAMPLE: "Joe Williams owes me $200 because he failed to pay for car repairs that he asked me to perform. I did all the repairs properly. Here is a work order signed by Joe authorizing me to do the work."

The fact that many contract cases are easy to win doesn't mean that all are. I have seen a good number of plaintiffs lose what to them seemed open and shut cases. Why? Simply because they failed to show the defendant owed them any money. Put another way: they failed to show that a contract existed (Example 2 below). In other situations the plaintiff

---

2 Leases and rental agreements, whether written or oral, are contracts. They are discussed in detail in the California Tenants' Handbook (Sixth Edition), Nolo Press (see back of this book).

is able to show that a contract existed, but not that the defendant breached it (Example 1 below).

EXAMPLE 1: Let's go over the facts of a situation that I witnessed recently in Small Claims Court in Oakland, California. Plaintiff sued defendant for $350, the cost of replacing a pigskin suede jacket that was ruined by defendant's cleaning establishment. Plaintiff had taken the jacket to defendant for cleaning and given him a $25 fee. Defendant, by accepting the jacket and the fee, clearly implied that he would properly clean the jacket. A contract existed.

Plaintiff was very sure of his loss. He stood in the courtroom, a great bear of a man, looking as if he had just escaped from a professional football team and slowly put the jacket on. As he wiggled into the coat, the whole courtroom, including the judge who almost choked trying to keep a straight face, burst out laughing. With a little luck the jacket would have fit a good-sized jockey. The sleeves barely came to the man's elbows and the coat itself didn't reach his waist.

As I sat watching, I thought that the case was over and that the plaintiff had won easily. Certainly by putting on the jacket he had made his point more effectively than he could have with ten minutes of testimony. I was wrong. The plaintiff had overlooked two things, one obvious, and one not so obvious. The defendant, a clever man, started his testimony and by the time he was done, the plaintiff's case had shrunk almost as much as the jacket.

The obvious thing that plaintiff overlooked in asking for the $350 replacement value of the jacket was that the jacket was two years old and had been worn a good bit. Valuation is a common problem in clothing cases and we discuss it in detail in Chapters 4 and 21. Let's just say here that the jacket was worth no more than $200 in its used condition and that, in any case where your property is damaged or destroyed, the amount of your recovery will be limited to the fair market value of the goods at the time the damage occurs--not their replacement value.

Now let's look at defendant's other defense. He testified that, when he saw the jacket after cleaning, he had been amazed. His cleaning shop specialized in leather goods and the process used should have resulted in no such shrinking problem. What's more, he testified that he had examined a number of other goods in the same cleaning batch and found no shrinking problem with any of them. To find out what happened, he sent the jacket to an "independent testing laboratory." Their report, which he presented to the court, stated that the problem was not in the cleaning, but in the jacket. It was poorly made in that the leather had been severely overstretched prior to assembly. When it had been placed in the cleaning fluid, it had shrunk as a result of this poor original workmanship.

What happened? The judge was convinced by the testing lab report and felt that defendant had breached no contract as far as the cleaning was concerned.[3] However, he also felt that defendant, as a leather cleaning specialist, had a responsibility to notify plaintiff that the jacket should not have been cleaned in the first place. Therefore, the judge held mostly for the defendant, but did award the plaintiff $50 in damages.

EXAMPLE 2: A few weeks later I saw another contract case where the plaintiff had suffered an obvious loss, but failed to show that defendant was responsible for making it good. This time it was a plaintiff landlord suing the parent of a tenant for damages that the tenant had done to her apartment. The parent was sued because he had co-signed his

---

3 Plaintiff could still bring suit against the person who made the jacket for defective workmanship. It could be argued that, by using inferior material, they had breached an implied warranty (contract) that the goods sold were reasonably fit.

daughter's lease contract. The plaintiff easily
convinced the judge that the damage had, in fact,
occurred and the judge seemed disposed toward giving
judgment for the $580 requested until the parent
presented his defense. He showed that the lease
between his daughter and the landlord had been
rewritten three times after he originally co-signed
the agreement without his again adding his signature.
He claimed that, because he had not co-signed any of
the subsequent lease contracts, he wasn't liable.
The judge agreed. The judge was probably relying on
the noteworthy case of Wexler v. McLucas, 48 CA 3
Supp 9 (1975). Leases, rental agreements and the
rights and responsibilities of co-signers are discussed in more detail in the California Tenants'
Handbook, Moskovitz, Warner and Sherman, Nolo Press.

NOTE: We will get into individual fact situations of contracts more in Chapter 16-21. Before you
decide whether or not you have a good case, read on.

══════◢◣══════

B. How to Approach a Case Where Your Property Has Been Damaged by the Negligent or Intentional Act of Someone Else

After cases involving breach of contract, the
most common disputes that come to Small Claims Court
involve damage to one person's property caused by the
negligent actions of another. Less often, the
plaintiff claims that he suffered loss because the
defendant intended to damage his belongings.

A technical definition of what constitutes
negligence could easily fill the next few pages.
Indeed, whole law texts have been written on the
subject. I remember thinking in law school that the
more scholarly professors wrote the more mixed up
they got. Like good taste or bad wine, negligence
seems to be easy to recognize, but hard to define.

Here is a one sentence definition. If, as a
result of another person's conduct, your property is
injured and that person didn't act with reasonable
care in the circumstances, you have a case based on
his negligence.[4] It's as simple--or complex--as
that. If you want to get into the gory details of
the subject, go to your nearest law library and get
any recent text on "Torts." "Torts" are wrongful
acts or injuries.

---

4 Sometimes negligence can occur when a person who has a duty or
responsibility to act fails to do so. For example, a car mechanic
who fails to check your brakes after promising to do so would be
negligent.

EXAMPLE: Jake knows the brakes on his ancient Saab are in serious need of repair, but does nothing about it. One night when the car is parked on a hill, the brakes fail and the car rolls across the street and destroys Carolyn's pomegranate tree. Carolyn sues Jake for $125.00, which is the reasonable value of the tree. Jake would lose because he did not act with reasonable care in the circumstances.

Another obvious situation involving negligence would be the car or bus that swerves into your driving lane and sideswipes your fender. The driver of the offending vehicle had a duty to operate it in such a way as to not harm you, and failed to do so. A situation where negligence could be difficult to show might involve your neighbor's tree that falls on a car parked in your driveway. Here you have to be ready to prove that for some reason (age, disease, an obviously bad root system, etc.) the tree was in a weakened condition, and the neighbor was negligent in failing to do something about it. If the tree had looked to be in good health, you would have a tough time proving that your neighbor was negligent in not cutting it down or propping it up.

There is no fool-proof way to determine in advance if someone is or is not negligent. It's often a close question--a matter of judgment. If you are in doubt, bring your case and let the judge decide. After all, he or she gets paid (by you) to do it.

Here are a couple of questions which may help you make a decision as to whether you have a good case based on someone else's negligence.

▼ Did the person whose act (or failure to act) injured you behave in a reasonable way? Or to put it another way, would you have behaved differently if you were in his or her shoes?

▼ Was your conduct partly the cause of the injury?

If you believe that the person who caused you to suffer a monetary loss behaved in an unreasonable way (ran a red light when drunk) and that you were acting sensibly (driving at 30 m.p.h. in the proper lane), you probably have a good case. If you were a little at fault (slightly negligent), but the other fellow was much more at fault (very negligent), you can still recover in California and most other states. If a judge finds that one person (drunk and speeding) was 80% at fault, and that the other (slightly inattentive) was 20% at fault, the comparatively innocent party can recover 60% of his or her loss.

C. How to Approach a Personal Injury Case

The considerations here are much the same as outlined in Section B just above. You must show not only that you were injured but that someone's intentional or negligent behavior caused your injury.[5]

EXAMPLE 1: Keija takes Harry, her Pekinese puppy, for a walk without a leash. Soto walks by and Harry takes an instant dislike to his purple and orange socks and shows it with a quick nip on Soto's right ankle. As Soto was on a public sidewalk where he had a right to be, we can safely assume that Keija was negligent in allowing Harry to bite him. Why? Because, as a society, we have decided that you can't let your dog run about biting people in public places even if they do have horrible taste in socks. If you do, you are negligent and are going to have to pay for it.

5 There is also a concept called "strict liability." This concept is applied to such things as nuclear reactors, munitions storage, people who keep wild and inherently dangerous animals (a cheetah in the city) and other extremely hazardous activities. Anyone injured by an inherently hazardous activity can recover without showing either negligence or intent to harm. This is because, when a high level of danger is present, the person undertaking the activity is "strictly liable" for any and all injuries.

EXAMPLE 2: Now, let's change our example and
assume that, instead of biting Soto, Harry went after
a burglar who was trying to sneak into Keija's garage
window. Let's also assume that after the dust
cleared and the cops hauled the burglar away it was
discovered that he had suffered the same injury as
Soto. Although the burglar's blood was just as red
as Soto's, he can recover nothing. Why? Because
Keija is entitled to protect herself and her property and as a society we have decided that keeping a
dog with sharp teeth is a reasonable way to do it.

EXAMPLE 3: Now let's change the example again.
This time Harry bites Walter, Keija's next-door neighbor, who had climbed over the backyard fence to get
some apples from Keija's tree. Keija knew that the
neighbor took the apples, but never encouraged him to
do so. The neighbor knew that Harry was in the yard
and that Harry's slogan seemed to be "if it moves,
bite it." Here again, there would be no liability.
Keija had taken reasonable precautions to secure
Harry in her own yard. She owed no duty of care to
her apple-poaching neighbor in this situation.

EXAMPLE 4: I know you're getting sick of hearing
about nasty little Harry, but bear with him a moment
longer. Let's assume now that Harry bites a
traveling carrot-peeler salesman who knocks at the
front door. Can the salesperson recover? Probably.
Even though Keija didn't invite him and never let a
carrot in the house, the salesperson had the right to
assume that it was safe to go up the walk to the
front door. But suppose Keija had a fence around the
front yard with a latched gate and a "Beware of the
Dog" sign, complete with a picture of Harry hanging
onto someone's leg? This would be enough to satisfy
Keija's duty of care to the rest of the world and if
the carrot-peeler salesman entered the gate anyway,
he would do so at his own risk.

SUGGESTION: Before you sue someone for a personal injury (or for property damage), think about whether they owed you a duty of care and whether they breached that duty. If in doubt, go ahead and sue, but be prepared to deal with this question ("liability") as well as simply showing the extent of your injury. In later chapters I will give you some practical advice as to how to prove your case.

---------------------------▲---------------------------

D. Stating Your Claim On Your Court Papers

Before you get too far into theories of law, let me bring you back to earth for a minute. While it is helpful to have a good grasp of what's involved in proving a contract or negligence case (the judge, after all, is a lawyer), it is also essential that you stay grounded on the facts of your grievance. One of the joys of Small Claims Court is that you don't plead theories of law--you state facts.

Let's jump ahead and take a look at the form you will fill out when you file your case. Turn to Chapter 10 and find the form entitled "Plaintiff's Statement." Look at Line 5. As you can see, there is little space for theory. Indeed, there is barely room to set down the facts of your dispute. You should state your case like this:

"I took my coat to John's Dry Cleaners and it was returned in a damaged (shrunk) condition."

"Defendant's dog bit me on the corner of Rose and Peach Streets in West Covina, California."

"The car repairs that Joe's Garage did on my car were done wrong, resulting in my engine burning."

"Defendant refused to return the cleaning deposit for my apartment even though I left it clean."

NOTE: When you state your case on the court papers, your only goal is to notify the other party and the court as to the broad outlines of your dispute. You don't want to try to argue the facts of your case or the law that you believe applies to it. Your chance to do this will come later in court.

IMPORTANT: Now is a good time to start organizing your materials in one place. Get a couple of manila envelopes or file folders, label them carefully, and find a safe place for storage. One folder or envelope should be used to store all documentary evidence such as receipts, letters, photographs, etc. The other is for your court papers, filing fee receipts, etc. It's no secret that more than one case has been won or lost because of good (or bad) record keeping.

3.

Can You Recover If You Win?

This is the shortest chapter in the book and the most important. In it, I ask all of you who are thinking of filing a Small Claims suit to focus on a very simple question--can you collect if you win? Collecting from many individuals or businesses isn't a problem as they are solvent and will routinely pay any judgments entered against them. But all too often, the main problem you face in Small Claims Court is not winning your case, but collecting your money when you do win.

I am co-author with Peter Jan Honigsberg of the book published by Nolo Press entitled The California Debtors' Handbook--Billpayers' Rights. It contains information for people who are over their heads in legal debts and don't know how they are going to keep the roof over their heads and clothes on their kids' backs. The message of the book is that, surprisingly, there are many ways for a debtor to protect

himself. A creditor can't take the food from the debtor's table, or the T.V. from his living room, or even the car from his driveway.[1]

What do these facts mean to you? Simply that many Californians who are not completely without money are nevertheless "judgment proof." You can sue them and get judgments against them until red cows dance on the yellow moon, but you can't collect a dime. Unfortunately, just this sort of frustrating thing happens every day--people go to lots of trouble to win cases only to realize that the judgment is uncollectable. This, of course, compounds the misery. Not only has the person suing lost the money from the original debt or injury, but also the time, trouble and expense of the Small Claims suit. As my grandmother used to say, "no one ever got to live in the big house on the hill by throwing a good quarter after a bad dime."

Whenever a dispute develops, it is all too easy to get caught up in thinking and arguing about who was wrong. So easy that perspective is lost and the problems of collection are forgotten. I emphasize this because I have so often observed people bringing cases to court in which there was never a hope of collecting. How can I tell ahead of time? I can't always, but in many situations, it's not hard. One thing I look for is whether or not the defendant is working. If a person fails to voluntarily pay a judgment, the easiest way to collect it is to garnish his or her wages. Thus, if the person sued is working, there is an excellent chance of collecting if payment is not made voluntarily. But you can't garnish a welfare, social security, unemployment, pension or disability check. So, if the person sued gets his income from one of these sources, red flags are flying.

---

1 A debtor's car is protected only if he has $500 or less equity in it, unless he uses the car as a tool of his trade, in which case the car is exempt from attachment as long as the equity is $2,500 or less. C.C.P. 690.4, 690.2.

But what about other assets? Can't a judgment be collected from sources other than wages? Yes, it can--bank accounts, motor vehicles and real estate are other common collection sources. But did you know that many types of property are exempt from attachment? Did you know that you can't effectively get at the equity in a family house unless it exceeds $45,000, or that a whole list of other possessions including furniture, a motor vehicle(s) with $1,200 in equity, the tools of a person's trade valued at $2,500, or at least 75% of wages are exempt?[2] So before you go down and file your papers ask yourself these questions:

1. Does the person you wish to sue voluntarily pay debts--or are you dealing with a person who will make it as difficult as possible to collect if you win?

2. Does he/she have a job?

3. If this person doesn't have a job, does he or she have some other means of support or assets that convince you that you can collect?

4. If you have your doubts about voluntary payment and the person you are suing doesn't have a job, can you identify some non-exempt assets that you can attach, such as a bank account, or real property other than the place where the person lives?

5. If a business is involved, is it solvent and does it have a good reputation for paying debts?

---

2 Each state has a list of "exempt" property. Check your state's statutes. In California, property that is exempt from being taken to satisfy debts is listed in the Code of Civil Procedure Section 704.010. Also, see the California Debtors' Handbook--Billpayers' Rights, Warner and Honigsberg, Nolo Press (order information at back of this book). The Debtors' Handbook contains forms and instructions necessary for a debtor to take advantage of his/her rights.

NOTE: If a person or a business declares bankruptcy and lists you as a creditor, your right to
recover is cut off. If you are owed money on a
secured debt (there was a security agreement as in
the case of a car or major appliance), you are
entitled to recover your security.

In Chapter 23, we deal in detail with the
mechanics of collecting after you get your judgment.
If you think that this may pose a problem, you will
wish to read this chapter now. But remember what my
canny, old grandmother said about bad dimes and good
quarters and don't waste your time chasing people who
have no money.

4.

How Much Can You Sue For?

The maximum amount you can sue for in Small Claims Court varies from state to state. In California it is $1,500. As I suggested in Chapter 1, if you are not in California, you should get the rules that affect you by calling your local Small Claims Court clerk. With minor exceptions Small Claims Court does not hear cases unless they are for money damages. This means that you can't use Small Claims Court to get a divorce, stop (enjoin) the city from cutting down your favorite oak tree, change your name, or do any of the thousands of other things that require some solution other than the payment of money. In California, Small Claims Court can also be used for certain types of evictions (see Chapter 20) and in rare situations, equitable relief (see Section D of this chapter).

Just because you have a claim which is less than the Small Claims maximum doesn't mean that you must sue in Small Claims Court. You can sue in Municipal (or Justice) Court on a $50 claim if you wish, but if you do, you must follow all their formal rules and pay filing fees that will average $25-$50. Unfortunately, this rule is often abused by businesses which file small cases in Municipal Court because it is harder for the non-lawyer to respond in a situation where formal pleadings are required. Accordingly, we favor legislation to require that all cases that can be brought in Small Claims Court be brought in that court.

Why is Small Claims Court limited to such small amounts and to cases involving money? Well, the traditional assumption has been that people aren't very competent to deal with their own legal affairs. Only lawyers, it was thought, were clever enough to handle anything but the most inconsequential claims. Who made these assumptions? We all have, but we have been encouraged to do so by lawyers themselves, who have long dominated our state legislatures where our court rules are made. Somehow, as a society, we have allowed lawyers to metamorphose from dry, little men in English villages with little more going for them than an ability to read and write and a fireprooff box in which to store papers, to self-proclaimed superpeople who seemed convinced they have been given a mandate to run the world. Small Claims Courts have been tolerated in part as a direct result of this growth in lawyers' egos. Lawyers have become so important in their own eyes that it is somehow beneath their dignity to become involved in disputes over piddling amounts.

But times are starting to change. All sorts of people are beginning to realize that our legal system is staggering under a heavy load of favoritism, waste, and archaic and often nonsensical rules designed primarily by and for lawyers. One result of this realization is a growing interest in expanding Small Claims Courts. In some states Small Claims Court jurisdiction has already been substantially increased. As you might guess, lawyers regard this expansion much as they would a 500-pound bear stepping slowly on their toes.

California, with its Small Claims maximum of $1,500, is about average.[1] If you are in a state where the amount is higher or lower, simply substitute your amount whenever you read $1,500 here. Knowing the largest amount for which you can sue is important, but it is only one of many facts that you will have to deal with in deciding how much you wish to demand when you fill out your papers. Here are some other things to think about.

A. Cutting Down a Claim That's Over the Limit to Fit Into Small Claims Court

It is legal to reduce an excessive claim so that it will fit into Small Claims Court. Thus, you could take a $2,100 debt and bring it into Small Claims Court, claiming only $1,500. But if you do this, you

---

1 Costs, such as filing fees, serving of process, fees where witnesses are subpoenaed, etc., are recoverable in addition to the $1,500 maximum.

forever waive the $600 difference between $1,500 and $2,100. In legal parlance, this is called "waiving the excess." Why wouldn't this be a silly thing to do? It would be if it weren't for the insanity of our court system where the alternative to Small Claims Court involves filing your suit in a formal court with dozens of complicated rules and the considerable expense involved in having a lawyer draw up papers, etc. A lawyer would probably charge considerably more than $600 to represent you. It is possible to represent yourself in Municipal or Superior Court, but doing so requires a good bit of homework and the guts to walk into an unfamiliar and sometimes hostile arena.[2] I don't mean to discourage you. Lots of people have successfully handled their cases in our formal courts, but you should be aware before you start that your path may be lonely and frustrating. If you wish to take your case to Municipal or Superior Court yourself, you might start by looking at a series of books entitled <u>California Forms</u>. This encyclopedia-like series shows you how to prepare most of the papers that you ever need to file.

B. Splitting Small Claims Court Cases

It is not legal to split an over-the-limit claim into two or more pieces to fit each into Small Claims Court. Taking the $2,100 figure we used above, this means you couldn't sue the same person separately for $1,100 and $1,000.[3] As with most rules, however, a little creative thought will take you a long way. While you can't split a case that's too big to get it

---

2 Law libraries exist in most major courthouses and are open to the public. Law librarians are usually very helpful in assisting you to find materials. See also, Elias, <u>Legal Research: How to Find and Understand the Law</u> (Nolo Press).

3 Defendant's claims that are over the $1,500 limit are discussed in Chapters 10 and 12.

into Small Claims Court, you can bring multiple suits against the same person as long as they are based on different claims. This is where the creativity comes in. There is often a large grey area in which it is genuinely difficult to differentiate between one divided claim and several independent ones. If you can reasonably argue that a $2,100 case actually involves two or more separate contracts, or injuries to your person or property, you may as well try dividing it. The worst that will happen is that a judge will disagree and tell you to make a choice between taking the entire claim to Municipal Court, or waiving any claim for money in excess of $1,500 and staying in Small Claims.

EXAMPLE 1: Recently I watched a man in the private telephone business come into Small Claims Court with three separate lawsuits against the same defendant for a combined total of $2,000. One, he said, was for failure to pay for phone installation, another was for failure to pay for phone maintenance and the third was for failure to pay for moving several phones to a different location. The man claimed that each suit was based on the breach of a separate contract. The judge, after asking a few questions, told the man that he was on the borderline between one divided (no good) and several separate (O.K.) claims, but decided to give him the benefit of the doubt and allowed him to present each case. The man won all three and got two judgments for $700 and a third for $600.

EXAMPLE 2: Another morning a woman alleged that she had lent a business acquaintance $1,000 twice and was therefore bringing two separate suits, each for $1,000. The defendant said that this wasn't true. She claimed that she had borrowed $2,000 to be repaid in two installments. A different judge, after listening to each person briefly, told the plaintiff that only one claim was involved and that, if she didn't want to waive all money over $1,500, she should go to Municipal Court.[4]

---

4 In the landlord-tenant area there is a ruling that a landlord must sue for all unpaid rent for a rental unit in one action and can't bring separate Small Claims suits based on each month's unpaid rent. Leske v. Municipal Court, 138 CA 3d 188.

SUGGESTION: If you wish to sue someone on two related claims, which you believe can be viewed as being separate, you may be better off to file your actions a few days apart. This will result in their being heard on different days, and in most metropolitan areas, by different judges. Unless the defendant shows up and argues that you have split one claim, you will likely get your judgments without difficulty. There is, however, one possible drawback to this approach. If you bring your claims in on the same day and the judge rules that they are one claim, he will give you a choice as to whether to waive the excess over $1,500 or go to Municipal Court. However, if you go to court on different days and the question of split claims is raised on the second or third day, you may have a problem. If the judge decides that your action in splitting the claims was improper, he has no choice but to throw the second and third claims out of court with no opportunity to refile in Municipal Court. This is because you have already sued and won and you are not entitled to sue the same person twice for the same claim.

C. How to Compute the Exact Amount of Your Claim

Sometimes it's easy to understand exactly what dollar amount to sue for, but it's often tricky. Before we get to the tricky part, let's go over the basic rule. When in doubt, always bring your suit a little on the high side. Why? Because the court has the power to award you less than you request, but can't give you more, even if the judge feels that you are entitled to it. But don't go overboard--if you sue for $1,500 on a $500 claim, you are likely to spur your opponent to furious opposition, ruin any chance for an out-of-court compromise, and lose the respect of the judge.

1. Computing the Exact Amount—Contract Cases

To arrive at the exact figure to sue on in contract cases, compute the difference between the amount you were supposed to receive under the contract and what you actually received. For example, if Jeannie Goodday agrees to pay Homer Brightspot $1,200 to paint her house to look like a rainbow, but then only gives him $800, Homer has a claim for $400 plus the cost of filing suit and serving Jeannie with the papers (costs are discussed in more detail in Chapter 15). The fact that Jeannie and Homer made their agreement orally does not bar Homer from suing. Oral contracts are O.K. as long as they can be carried out in a year. Of course, people tend to remember oral contracts differently and this can lead to serious proof problems once you get to court. It is always wise to reduce agreements to writing, even if only to a note or letter agreement dated and signed by both parties.

Where the contract involves lending money in exchange for interest, don't forget to include the interest due in the amount you sue for.[5] I have seen several disappointed people sue for the exact amount of the debt (say $500) and not include interest (say $50), thinking that they could have the judge add the interest when they got to court. This can't be done --the judge doesn't have the power to make an award larger than the amount you request.[6] Of course, you can't sue for interest if the interest amount would make your claim larger than the Small Claims maximum.

---

[5] As a general rule, you can only recover interest when it is called for in a written or oral contract. If you loaned a friend $100, but never mentioned interest, you can sue only for the return of the $100.

[6] If you find yourself in court and realize you have asked for too little, you should request that the judge allow you to amend your claim. Some judges will do this and offer the defendant a continuance to deal with defending against the higher amount if they wish it.

Unfortunately, not all claims based on breach of contract are easy to reduce to a money amount. This is often due to a legal doctrine known as "mitigation of damages." Don't let the fancy term throw you. Like so much of our law the concept behind the "mumbo jumbo" is simple. "Mitigation of damages" means simply that the person bringing suit for breach of contract must himself take all reasonable steps to limit the amount of damages he suffers. Let's take an example from the landlord-tenant field. Tillie the tenant moves out three months before the end of her lease (remember a lease is a contract). Her monthly rent is $350. Can Lothar the landlord recover the full $1,050 ($350 x 3 months) from Tillie in Small Claims Court? Probably not. Why? Because Lothar has control of the empty apartment and must take reasonable steps to attempt to find a new tenant. If Lothar can re-rent the apartment to someone else for $350 or more per month, he has suffered no damage. Put another way, if Lothar re-rents the apartment, he has fulfilled his responsibility to "mitigate damages." In a typical situation it might take Lothar several weeks (unless he had plenty of advance notice, or Tillie herself found a new tenant) to find a suitable new tenant. If it took three weeks and $25 worth of newspaper ads, Lothar could recover approximately $300 from Tillie.

The "mitigation of damages" concept isn't only applicable to landlord-tenant situations, but applies to every contract case where the person damaged can take reasonable steps to protect himself or herself. In the earlier example, if Jeannie Goodday had agreed to pay Homer Brightspot $100 per day for seven days to paint her house and then had cancelled after the first day, Homer could sue her for the remaining $600, but, if he did, he would surely be asked whether he had earned any other money during the six days. If he had, it would be subtracted from the $600. But what if Homer refused other work and slept in his hammock all week? If Jeannie could show that he had turned down other jobs, or had refused to make reasonable efforts to seek available work, this too would be used to reduce Homer's recovery.

SUGGESTION: Sue only for the amount of money you are out. Don't try to collect money in court that you have already recovered from someone else.

2. Computing the Exact Amount—Property Damage Cases

When your property has been damaged by the negligent or intentional act of someone else, you have a right to recover for your loss.[7] This amount is often, but not always, the amount of money that it would take to fix the damaged item.

EXAMPLE: John Quickstop bashes into Melissa Caretaker's new Dodge, smashing in the left rear. How much can Melissa recover? The amount that it would cost to fix, or, if necessary, replace the damaged part of her car. Melissa should get several estimates from responsible body and fender shops and sue for the amount of the lowest one, if John won't pay voluntarily (see Chapter 19).

There is, however, a big exception to the rule that a person who has had property damaged can recover the cost of fixing the damaged item. This occurs when the cost to fix the item exceeds its actual cash market value. You are not entitled to a new or better object--only to have your loss made good. Had Melissa Caretaker been driving a 1961 Dodge, the cost to fix the fender might well have exceeded the value of the car. If this were the case, she would be entitled to the value of the car, not the value of the fender repair.

---

7 If you haven't already done so, read Chapter 2. It is important to remember that you not only have to establish the amount of your damage, but that the person you are suing is legally responsible ("liable") to pay your damages.

Think of it this way. In any situation where the value of the repair exceeds the value of the object, you are limited to the fair market value of the object (what you could have sold it for) a minute before the damage occurred. From this figure, you have to subtract the value, if any, of the object after the injury. Of course, in deciding how much to claim, you should give yourself the benefit of the doubt as to how much a piece of property is worth, but don't be ridiculous. A $300 motor scooter might conceivably be worth $450 or $500 but it's not worth $750.

EXAMPLE: Let's return to Melissa. If her 1961 Dodge was worth $700 and the fender would cost $800 to replace, she would be limited to a $700 recovery, less what the car could be sold for in its damaged state. If this was $50 for scrap, she would be entitled to $650. However, if Melissa had just gotten a new engine and transmission and her car was worth $1,200, she would legally be entitled to recover and sue for the entire $800 needed to get her Dodge fixed.

NOTE: Many people insist on believing that they can recover the cost of getting a replacement object when theirs has been totalled. As you should now understand, this isn't necessarily true. If Melissa's $700 car was totalled and she claimed that she simply couldn't get another decent car for less than $900, she would still be limited to recovering $700. To get $900 she would have to show that her car had a sale value of that much just before the accident. This rule can cause you a real hardship when an older object that is in great shape is destroyed. The fair market value may be low, while the cost of replacement high.

Knowing what something is worth and proving it are quite different. A car that you are sure is worth $800 may look like it's only worth $500 to someone else. In court you will want to be prepared to show that your piece of property is worth every bit of the $800. Perhaps the best way to do this is

to get some estimates (opinions) from experts in the
field (i.e., a car dealer if your car was ruined).
This is best done by having the expert come to court
and testify, but can also be done in writing. You
will also want to check newspaper and flea market ads
for the prices asked for comparable goods and creatively explore any other approaches that make sense
given the type of damage you have suffered. We talk
more about proving your case in court in Chapters
16-21.

3. Computing the Exact Amount—Cases Involving Damage to Clothing

THIS, YOUR HONOR WAS MY BEST JACKET PRIOR TO ITS VISIT TO ACME CLEANERS...

Clothing is property so why am I separating it
out for special treatment? For two reasons. Cases
involving clothing are extremely common in Small
Claims Court and judges seem to apply a logic to them
that they apply to no other property damage cases.
The reason for this is that clothing is personal to
its owner and often has small or little value to
anyone else even though it may be in good condition.

If the rules that we just learned (i.e., you can recover the repair cost of a damaged item unless this would be more than its market value before the damage occurred, in which case you are limited to recovering its total value) were strictly applied to clothing, there would often be little or no recovery. This is because there is not much market for used clothing.

When suing for damage to new or almost new clothing, sue for its cost. If it is older, sue for that percentage of the value of the clothing which reflects how worn it was when the damage occurred. For example, if your two-year-old suit which cost $400 new were destroyed, sue for $200 if you feel the suit would have lasted another two years. In clothing cases most judges want answers to these questions: How much did the clothing cost originally? How much of its useful life was consumed at the time the damage occurred? Does the damaged item still have some value to the owner, or has it been ruined?

EXAMPLE 1: Wendy took her new $250 coat to Rudolph, a tailor, to have alterations made. Rudolph cut part of the back of the coat in the wrong place and ruined it. How much should Wendy sue for? $250 as the coat was almost new. She could probably expect to recover close to this amount.

EXAMPLE 2: The same facts as just above but the coat was two years old and had been well worn. Here Wendy would be wise to sue for $200 and hope to recover $150.

EXAMPLE 3: Again Wendy and the coat. This time we will return it to its almost new condition, but have Rudolph slightly deface the back, instead of completely destroying it. I would still advise Wendy to sue for the full $250. Whether she could recover that much would depend on the judge. Most would probably award her a little less on the theory that the coat retained some value. Were I Wendy, however, I would strongly argue that I didn't buy the coat with the expectation that I could only wear it in a closet and that, as far as I was concerned, the coat was ruined. (See Chapter 21 for more detail if you are arguing a clothing case in Small Claims Court.)

4. Computing the Exact Amount—Personal Injury Cases

Lawyers quickly take over the great majority of cases where someone is injured. These claims are routinely inflated (a sprained back might be worth $3,000-$5,000 or more), because it is in everyone's selfish interest to do so. The insurance adjusters and insurance company lawyers are as much a part of this something-for-nothing syndrome, as are the ambulance-chasing plaintiff's attorneys. If there aren't lots of claims, lots of lawsuits, lots of depositions and negotiations, it wouldn't take lots of people making money to run the system. Even in states with so-called "no-fault" automobile insurance, the dispute resolution bureaucracy has managed to protect itself very well.

Some small personal injury cases do get to Small Claims Court, however. Dog bite cases are one common example and there are others. Here is how you figure the amount to sue for:

Out of pocket medical costs,
including medical transportation   _____

Loss of pay, or vacation time
for missing work   _____

Pain and Suffering[8]   _____

TOTAL[9]   _____

[8] In more serious cases you would also have to figure the monetary value of any permanent injury. These cases do not, however, get to Small Claims Court. Also, contrary to the erroneous "advice" many Small Claims clerks give, you can sue for pain and suffering expenses, the same as you can in regular Municipal or Superior Court. The only limitation is that the amount you can sue for is $1,500. See Leuschen v. Small Claims Court (1923) 191 Cal. 133 and 59 Cal. Os. Atty. Gen. 321 (1976).

[9] Often a personal injury is accompanied by injury to property. Thus, a dog bite might also ruin your pants. You add all of your damages together as part of the same suit. You can't sue separately for your pants and your behind.

Medical and hospital bills including transportation to and from the doctor are routinely recoverable as long as you have established that the person you are suing is at fault. However, if you are covered by health insurance and the insurance company has already paid your medical costs, you will find that your policy says that any money that you recover for these costs must be turned over to the company. Often, insurance companies don't make much effort to keep track of, or recover, Small Claims judgments as the amounts of money involved don't make it worthwhile. Knowing this, many judges are reluctant to grant judgments for medical bills unless the individual can show that they are personally out-of-pocket the money.

Loss of pay or vacation time is viewed in a similar way. If the cocker spaniel down the block lies in wait for you behind a hedge and grabs a piece of your derriere for breakfast, and as a result you miss a day of work getting yourself patched up, you are entitled to recover the loss of any pay, commissions or vacation time. However, if you are on a job with unlimited paid sick time, so that you suffer no loss for missing work, you have nothing to recover.

The third area of recovery is for what is euphemistically known as "pain and suffering." This is a catch-all phrase that simultaneously means a great deal and nothing at all. Generations of lawyers have made a good living mumbling it. Their idea is often to take a minor injury (sprained ankle) and inflate its value as much as possible by claiming that the injured party underwent great "pain and suffering." "How much is every single minute that my poor client suffered an unbearably painful ankle worth—$1.00, $5.00, $10,000?" etc. When you read about million dollar settlements, a good chunk of the recovery routinely falls into the "pain and suffering" category. I don't mean to suggest that recovery for "pain and suffering" is always wrong—just that it is often abused.

But back to the case of the nasty cocker spaniel. If you received a painful bite, spent the morning getting your rump attended to, had to take several pain killers and then make sure that the dog was free of rabies, you would very likely feel that you were entitled to some recovery. One judge I know doesn't pay much attention to the evidence in this type of case. He simply awards $250 for a bite by a medium-sized dog, adds $100 for anything the size of a lion, and subtracts $100 if the dog looks like a mouse.

SUGGESTION: In thinking about how much you wish to sue for, be aware that lawyers often bring suit for three to four times the amount of the out-of-pocket damages (medical bills and loss of work). Therefore, if you were out of pocket $150, you might wish to ask for $500, the overage being for "pain and suffering." If you have no medical bills (there is no blood or at least x-rays), you will find it difficult to recover anything for "pain and suffering." This is why lawyers routinely encourage their clients to get as much medical attention as possible. Or as my friend Anne-Therese says, "The squeaky wheel gets the grease."

EXAMPLE 1: Mary Tendertummy is drinking a bottle of pop when a mouse foot floats to the surface. She is greatly nauseated, loses her lunch and goes to the doctor for medication. As a result, she loses an afternoon's pay. She sues the pop company for $500. This is reasonable. She will probably recover most of this amount.

EXAMPLE 2: The same thing happens to Roy Toughguy. He just throws the pop away in disgust and goes back to work. A few weeks later he hears about Mary's recovery and decides that he too could use $500. How much is he likely to recover? Probably not much more than the price of the soda--he apparently suffered little or no injury.

NOTE: Certain costs of suit such as filing fees, subpoenaed witness fees, costs of serving papers, etc., can be recovered, but many, such as compensation for time off from work to go to court, transportation to and from court, etc., cannot. See Chapter 15 for more information. You do not add costs to the amount of your suit. The judge does this when the case is decided.

======▲▽▲======

D. Equitable Relief (or Money Can't Always Solve the Problem)

Nearly half the states, including California, allow judges to grant relief (providing you ask for it) in ways that do not involve the payment of money, if equity (fairness) demands it. In California (Code of Civil Procedure Section 116.3), "equitable relief" is limited to one or more of four categories: "recission," "restitution," "reformation," and "specific performance." Let's translate these into English.

RECISSION: This is a remedy that is used when a grossly unfair or fraudulent contract is discovered or where a contract was based on a mistake as to an important fact. Thus, if a merchant sued you for failure to pay for aluminum siding that you contended had been misrepresented and was a total rip-off, you could ask that the contract be rescinded.

RESTITUTION: This is an important remedy. It gives a judge the power to order that a particular piece of property be transferred to its original owner when fairness requires that the contracting parties be restored to their original positions. It could be used in the common situation in which one person sells another a piece of property (say a motor scooter) and the other fails to pay. Instead of simply giving the seller a money judgment which might be hard to collect, the judge now has the power to order the scooter restored to its original owner.

REFORMATION: This remedy is somewhat unusual.
It has to do with changing (reforming) a contract to
meet the original intent of the parties in a situation where some term or condition agreed to by the
parties has been left out and where fairness dictates
that this be done. Thus, if Arthur the Author and
Peter the Publisher orally agree that Peter will
publish Arthur's 200-page book and then they write a
contract inadvertently leaving out the number of
pages, a court would very likely "reform" the contract to include this provision if Arthur showed up
with a 750-page manuscript. Reformation is most
commonly used when an oral agreement is written down
incorrectly.

SPECIFIC PERFORMANCE: This is an important
remedy that comes into play where a contract
involving an unusual or "one-of-a-kind" object has
not been carried out. Say you agree to buy a unique
antique jade ring for your mother's birthday that is
exactly like the one she lost years before, and then
the seller refuses to go through with the deal. A
court could cite the doctrine of "specific performance" to order that the ring be turned over to you.
"Specific performance" will only be ordered in situations where the payment of money will not make a
party to a contract whole.

NOTE: In filling out your court papers, you
will still be required to indicate that the value of
the item for which you want equitable relief is under
the Small Claims maximum. Thus, you might describe
the nature of your claim (Chapter 10, Step 1) as
follows: "I want the delivery of a 'one-of-a-kind'
antique jade ring worth approximately $700 according
to my contract with defendant."

Oops! It's sometimes difficult to get court clerks to understand what you mean when you ask for equitable relief--indeed, most that we have talked to haven't developed any forms to handle these claims and quite a few had never even heard of the possibility of a Small Claims Court judge being able to grant "equitable relief." So, if you run into reactions that border on disbelief when you ask if equitable relief remedies are possible, refer the clerk (and maybe even the judge) to Section 116.3 of the Code of Civil Procedure and remind the judge that he or she does have the power to grant equitable relief.

5.

Is the Suit Brought Within the Proper Time Limits (Statute of Limitations)?

Each state sets up time limits within which lawsuits must be filed. These are called Statutes of Limitations. Time limits are different for different types of cases. If you wait too long, your right to sue will be barred by these statutes. Why have a Statute of Limitations? Because it has been found that disputes are best settled soon after they develop. Unlike wine, lawsuits don't improve with age. Memories fade and witnesses die or move away, and once-clear details tend to blur together. As a general rule, it is wise to sue as soon after your dispute arises as is reasonably possible. Statutes of Limitations are almost never less than one year, so if you file promptly, you should have little to worry about.

A. California Statute of Limitations Periods [1]

PERSONAL INJURY: One year from the injury, or, if the injury was not immediately discovered, one year from the date it was discovered.

ORAL CONTRACTS: Two years from the day the contract was broken.

WRITTEN CONTRACTS: Four years from the date of breach of contract.

DAMAGE TO PERSONAL OR REAL PROPERTY: Three years from the date the damage occurs.

FRAUD: Three years from the date of the discovery of the fraud.

SUITS AGAINST PUBLIC AGENCIES: Before you can sue a city, county or the state government, you must file an administrative claim form. The time period in which this must be done is normally 100 days. This is not precisely a Statute of Limitations, but it has the same effect. (See Chapter 8 for a more complete discussion of how to sue governments in Small Claims Court.)

NOTE: Some contracts which you may assume to be oral may actually be written. People often forget that they signed papers when they first arranged for goods or services. For example, your charge accounts, telephone service, insurance policies as well as most major purchases of goods and services involve a written contract, even though you haven't signed any papers for years. And another thing--to have a written contract you need not have signed a document full of "whereas's" and therefores. Any

▼

1 I only include the most common Statutes of Limitations periods here. You will find the rest in California C.C.P. Sections 312-363.

signed writing can be a contract even if it's written on toilet paper with lipstick. When you go to a car repair shop and they make out a work order and you sign it—that's a contract. (See Chapter 2 for more about contracts.)

If you live outside of California, you will wish to check your states's Statute of Limitations periods if any considerable time has passed between the time an incident occurred and the time you file suit. You will find a set of your state's laws at a public library or a law library which you will find located at the local courthouse. Check the index under "Statute of Limitations" or just "Limitations." If you have trouble finding what you need, ask the librarian for help. Librarians positively enjoy finding things.

B. Computing the Statute of Limitations

OK, now let's assume that you have found out what the relevant limitations period is. How do you know what date to start your counting from? That's easy. Start with the day the injury to your person or property occurred, or, if a contract is involved, start with the day that the failure to perform under the terms of the contract occurred. Where a contract to pay in installments is involved, start with the day that the first payment was missed.[2]

EXAMPLE: Doolittle owes Crabapple $500, payable in five monthly installments of $100. Both live in San Jose, California. They never wrote down any of the terms of their agreement. Doolittle misses his third monthly payment which was due on January 1,

---

2 The Statute of Limitations (four years on a written contract) applies separately to each installment of a contract. Thus, if you agree to pay $5,000 in five installments commencing January 1, 1985 and continuing on January 1 of each succeeding year and never waive the Statute of Limitations, your first payment will be barred by the statute on January 2, 1989, if you fail to pay it, unless, of course, the creditor sues you first. However, your second payment will not be barred until January 2, 1990.

1983. Crabapple should compute his Statute of Limitations period from January 2, 1983, assuming, of course, that Doolittle doesn't later catch up on his payments. Since the Statute of Limitations for oral contracts is two years, this means that Crabapple has until January 1, 1985 to file his suit. If a written contract had been involved, Crabapple could file until January 1, 1987, as the Statute of Limitations on written contracts is four years.

I am frequently asked to explain the legal implications of the following situation. After the Statute of Limitations runs out (say two years on an oral contract to pay for having a fence painted), the debtor commences voluntarily to make payments. Does the voluntary payment have the effect of creating a new two-year Statute of Limitations period, allowing the person who is owed the money to sue if the debtor again stops paying? In most states including California, simply starting to pay on an obligation barred by the Statute of Limitations doesn't create a new period for suit.[3] All the creditor can do is to keep his toes crossed and hope that the debtor's belated streak of honesty continues. However, if the debtor signs a written agreement to make the payments, this does create a new Statute of Limitations period. In legal slang, this is called "reaffirming the debt."

EXAMPLE: Back to the drama of Doolittle and Crabapple. Let's assume that in February, 1983, Doolitle experiences a burst of energy, gets a job and decides to pay off all of his old debts. He sends Crabapple $50. A week later, suffering terrible strain from getting up before noon, he quits his job and reverts to his old ways of sleeping in the sun when not reading the racing form. Is the Statute of Limitations allowing Crabapple to sue reinstated? No. As we learned above, once the limitation period of two years has run out, it can't be revived by simply making a payment. However, if Doolittle had sent Crabapple the $50 and had also

---

3 See California Code of Civil Procedure Section 360.

included a letter saying that he would pay the remainder of the debt, Crabapple would again be able to sue and get a judgment if he failed to pay. Why? Because a written promise to pay a debt barred by the Statute of Limitations has the legal effect of reestablishing the debt.

DEBTOR'S NOTE: If a creditor and debtor discuss an unpaid bill and the creditor agrees to give the debtor more time to pay, to lower payments, or make some other accommodation, the debtor will almost always be asked to waive the Statute of Limitations. The Statute of Limitations on a written contract is four years. Code of Civil Procedure Section 360.5 allows the statute to be waived for an additional four-year period by written agreement.

C. Telling the Judge That the Statute of Limitations Has Run Out

What should a defendant do if he believes that the Statute of Limitations period has run out? Tell the judge. Sometimes a judge will figure this out without a reminder, but sometimes he won't. If you are a defendant, don't ever assume that because the clerk has filed the papers and you have been properly served, this means that the plaintiff has started his or her suit on time. The clerk never gets involved in Statute of Limitations questions. They will cheerfully file a suit brought on a breach of contract occurring in 1916.

6.

How to Settle Your Dispute

Litigation should be a last, not a first, resort. Suing is not as bad as shooting, but neither is it as much fun as a good back rub. Rarely does anyone have a high time in court. In addition to being time-consuming and emotionally draining, lawsuits tend to polarize disagreements into "win all, lose all" propositions where face (and pocketbook) saving compromise is difficult. Most of us are terrified of making fools of ourselves in front of strangers. When forced to defend our actions in a public forum, we tend rather regularly to adopt a most self-righteous view of our own conduct, and to attribute the vilest of motives to our opponents. Many of us are willing to admit that we have been a bit of a fool in private--especially if the other person does too--but in public, we will stonewall all the way, even when it would be to our advantage to appear a little more fallible.

I have witnessed dozens of otherwise sensible people litigate the most appalling trivia including one case in which the parties effectively tied up over $2,000 of each other's property (and had a fist fight) over a fishing pole worth $15. This doesn't mean that I don't think you should pursue your case to court if necessary. What I am suggesting is this: before you file your case, ask yourself whether you have done everything reasonably possible (and then a little more) to try to settle the case.

A. Try to Talk Your Dispute Out

Making an attempt to settle your case isn't a waste of time. Indeed, you are required to make the attempt. The law in many states including California states that a "demand" for payment be made prior to filing a court action. Increasingly the "demand" requirement is being interpreted to mean that the "demand" be in the form of a letter.

But first things first. Before you reach for pen and paper, try to talk to the person with whom you are having the dispute. I can't count how many times clients have consulted me about supposedly insurmountable disputes in situations where they had never once tried to talk it out with the other person.[1] Apparently many of us have a strong psychological barrier to talking to people we are upset with, especially if we have already exchanged heated words. Sometimes we seem to think that a willingness to compromise shows weakness. But wasn't it Winston Churchill who said, "I would rather jaw, jaw, jaw than war, war, war"?

---

1 Just before making final revisions on this chapter, I sat as judge pro tem in a case where one man sued another for $500 resulting from a car accident. The defendant was "willing to pay," he said. "Why haven't you paid before?" I asked. "No one asked me to," he replied.

IMPORTANT: An offer of compromise made either orally or in writing does not bind the person making the offer to that amount if the compromise is not accepted. Thus, you could make an original demand for $500, then offer to compromise for $350, and, if your compromise offer was turned down, still sue for $500.

If you take my advice and again try to talk things out with your opponent and are successful, write down your agreement. Oral understandings, especially between people who have small confidence in one another, are often not worth the breath used to speak them out. Here are two sample compromise forms that you may be able to adopt to your uses.

SAMPLE AGREEMENT 1

Dusty Rider and Bigshot Owner agree as follows:

1. Dusty was to exercise Bigshot's horses every morning for two weeks from October 1 to October 15 at Golden Gate Fields Racetrack in Albany, California, and was to be paid $15 per horse exercised each morning;

2. Bigshot's horses got sick on September 29 and there was no need for Dusty's services;

3. Dusty gave up other employment to make herself available to ride Bigshot's horses, and she couldn't find another riding job at short notice;

4. Dusty and Bigshot agree that $600 is fair compensation for her loss of work and Dusty agrees to accept this amount as a complete settlement of all of her claims.

_____	_____
Date	Dusty Rider
_____	_____
Date	Bigshot Owner

SAMPLE AGREEMENT 2

Walter Spottedhound and Nellie Neighbor agree that Walter's "mixed breed" black dog Clem sneaked onto Nellie's patio and bit her behind the right knee. After taking into consideration Nellie's medical bills, the fact that she had to miss two hours' work while at the doctor's office, and the pain and discomfort she has suffered, it is agreed that Walter will pay her

---

$250 in full settlement of all her claims. The money will be paid in five equal monthly installments. The first installment is hereby paid this date and the next four will be paid on the first day of February, March, April and May.

It is also agreed that Walter will commence at once to construct a fence to keep Clem out of Nellie's yard.

_____	_____
Date	Walter Spottedhound
_____	_____
Date	Nellie Neighbor

B. Write a "Demand" Letter

If your efforts to talk your problems out fail (or despite my urging you refuse to try), your next step is to send your adversary a letter. As noted above, many courts require that a "demand" letter be sent. But even if there is no such requirement, it is almost essential that you send one. Why? Simple--the "demand" letter is not only useful in trying to settle your case, it is your best opportunity to lay your case before the judge in a carefully organized way. In a sense, it allows you to manufacture evidence that you will be permitted to use in court if the case isn't settled. Either way, you can't lose, so take the time to write a good letter.

Your letter should be reasonably short, directly to the point, and, above all, polite (you catch more flies with honey than by hitting them over the head with a mallet). Use a typewriter and keep a carbon or photocopy. Limit your remarks to a page, or at most, a page and a half. Remember, if the case doesn't settle, you will want to show the letter to the judge--and what's more important, you will want the judge to read it. It's my experience that aside from letters of the heart, no one ever reads much more than a page with anything like attention.

Remember, the judge doesn't know anything about how your problem started and developed. This means that you will want to write the letter so that it briefly reviews the entire dispute. It may seem a little odd, writing all the facts for your opponent who well knows them, and it may result in a formal sounding letter. So what? You want to produce a result that the judge can understand.

Let's consider a case I watched in Los Angeles one morning. The facts (with a little editorial license) were simple. Jennifer moved into Peter's house in August, agreeing to pay $150 per month rent. The house had four bedrooms, each occupied by one person. The kitchen and other common areas were shared. Things went well enough until one chilly evening in October when Jennifer turned on the heat. Peter was right behind her to turn it off, explaining that heat inflamed his allergies.

As the days passed and fall deepened, heat became more and more of an issue until one cold, late November night when Jennifer returned home from her waitress job to find her room "about the same temperature as the inside of an icicle." After a short cry, she started packing and moved out the next morning. She refused to pay Peter any additional rent, claiming that she was within her rights to terminate her month-to-month tenancy without giving notice because the house was uninhabitable.[2] It took Peter one month to find a suitable tenant and to have that person move in. Therefore, he was without a tenant for one month and lost rent in the amount of $150.

After calling Jennifer several times and asking her to make good the $150 only to have her slam down the phone in disgust, Peter wrote her the following letter:

---

2 In California, tenants do have the right to simply leave, or in the alternative, to stay and cease paying rent, if conditions in their rented home become uninhabitable, whether the cause is no heat, water, electricity, etc. See the California Tenants' Handbook, Moskovitz, Warner and Sherman, Nolo Press (order information at the back of this book).

```
                              61 Spring St.
                              Los Angeles, Calif.

                              January 1, 19__


Jennifer Tenant
111 Sacramento St.
Palos Verdes, Calif.

Dear Jennifer:

     You are a real idiot.  Actually you're worse than that: you're malici-
ous - walking out on me before Christmas and leaving me with no tenant
when you know that I needed the money to pay my child support.  You know
that I promised to get you an electric room heater.  Don't think I don't
know that the real reason you moved out was to live with your boyfriend.

     Please send me the $150 I lost because you didn't give me a month's
notice like the law says you are supposed to.  If you don't, I will sue
you.


                              In aggravation,


                              Peter Landperson
```

To which Jenifer replied:

```
                              111 Sacramento St.
                              Palos Verdes, Calif.

                              January 4, 19__


Peter Landperson
61 Spring St.
Los Angeles, Calif.

Dear Mr. Landperson:

     You nearly froze me to death, you cheap bastard.  I am surprised it
only took a month to rent that iceberg of a room - you must have found
a rich polar bear (ha ha).  People like you should be locked up.

     I hope you choke on an ice cube.


                              Jennifer Tenant
```

As you have no doubt guessed, both Peter and Jennifer made similar mistakes. Instead of being business-like, each deliberately set out to annoy the other, reducing any possible chance of compromise. In addition, they each assumed that they were writing only to the other, forgetting about the judge. Thus, both lost a valuable chance to present the judge with a coherent summary of the facts as they saw them. As evidence in a subsequent court proceeding, both letters were worthless.

(Now let's interrupt these proceedings and give Peter and Jennifer another chance to write sensible letters.)

> 61 Spring St.
> Los Angeles, Calif.
>
> January 1, 19_
>
> Jennifer Tenant
> 111 Sacramento St.
> Palos Verdes, Calif.
>
> Dear Jennifer:
>
> As you will recall, you moved into my house at 61 Spring St., Los Angeles, California, on August 1, 1978, agreeing to pay me $150 per month rent on the first of each month. On November 29 you suddenly moved out, having given me no advance notice whatsoever.
>
> I realize that you were unhappy about the fact that the house was a little on the cool side, but I don't believe that this was a serious problem as the temperature was at all times over 60° and I had agreed to get you an electric heater for your room by December.
>
> I was unable to get a tenant to replace you (although I tried every way I could and asked you for help) until January 1, 1979. This means that I am short $150 rent for the room you occupied. If necessary, I will take this dispute to court because, as you know, I am on a very tight budget. I hope that this isn't necessary and that we can arrive at a sensible compromise. I have tried to call you with no success. Perhaps you can give me a call in the next week to talk this over.
>
> Sincerely,
>
> Peter Landperson

To which our now enlightened Jennifer promptly replied:

```
                                    111 Sacramento St.
                                    Palos Verdes, Calif.

                                    January 4, 19_


     Peter Landperson
     61 Spring St.
     Los Angeles, Calif.

     Dear Peter:

         I just received your letter concerning the rent at 61 Spring St. and
     am sorry to say that I don't agree either with the facts as you have pre-
     sented them, or with your demand for back rent.

         When I moved in August 1, 1978, you never told me that you had an al-
     lergy and that there would be a problem keeping the house at a normal
     temperature.  I would not have moved in had you informed me of this.

         From early October when we had the first cool evenings, all through
     November (almost 2 months), I asked that you provide heat.  You didn't.
     Finally it became unbearable to return from work in the middle of the
     night to a cold house which was often below 60°.  It is true that I
     moved out suddenly, but I felt that I was within my rights under Calif-
     ornia law which states that a tenant need not pay rent for an uninhab-
     itable space (see the California Tenants' Handbook, Moskovitz, Warner
     and Sherman).

         Since you mentioned the non-existent electric heater in your letter,
     let me respond to that.  You first promised to get the heater over a
     month before I moved out and never did.  Also, as I pointed out to you
     on several occasions, the heater was not a complete solution to the
     problem as it would have heated only my room and not the kitchen, liv-
     ing room, dining area, etc.  You repeatedly told me that it would be im-
     possible to heat these areas.

         Peter, I sincerely regret the fact that you feel wronged, but I be-
     lieve that I have been very fair with you.  I am sure that you would
     have been able to re-rent the room promptly if the house had been warm.
     I regret that I don't believe that any compromise is possible and that
     you will just have to go to court if that's what you wish to do.


                                    Sincerely,



                                    Jennifer Tenant
```

As you can see, while the second two letters are less fun to read, they are far more informative. Both Peter and Jennifer have clearly set forth their positions. The goal of reaching an acceptable compromise was not met, but both have prepared a good statement of their positions for the judge. Of course, in court, both Peter and Jennifer will testify, present witnesses, etc. in addition to their letters, but court proceedings are often rushed and confused and it's nice to have something for the judge to fall back on. Be sure to bring the carbon

copy (or photocopy) of your demand letter to court
when your case is to be heard. Be sure, too, that the
judge is given the copy as part of your case. The
judge won't be able to guess that you have it; you
will have to let him or her know and hand it to the
clerk. (For more about what happens in court, see
Chapters 13-15.)

IMPORTANT: If you compromise your case after
you have filed it in court, but before the court
hearing, be sure to do so in writing. Also let the
court know that you won't be appearing. Some courts
will ask that the plaintiff sign a "Request for Dismissal" form. Never do this unless your compromise
agreement has already been reduced to writing. Also,
it is not wise to have a case dismissed unless you
have been paid in full. If the compromise settlement involves installment payments, it would be wise
to go to court and present it to the judge. He or
she can then enter a judgment in the same terms as
the compromise. If this is done and then the
judgment is not paid, it can be collected using the
techniques discussed in Chapter 24.

C. Settlement at Court

Sometimes cases are settled in court while you are waiting for your case to be heard. It is perfectly proper to ask the other person if he or she wishes to step into the hall for a moment to talk the matter over. If you can agree on a compromise, wait until the case is called and tell the judge the amount you have agreed upon and whether the amount is to be paid all at once, or over time. The judge can either order the case dismissed if one person pays the other on the spot, or can enter a judgment for the amount that you have compromised upon, if payment is to be made later.

D. Mediation as an Alternative

Here at Nolo Press we are enthusiastic about the recent trend away from the adversary approach to dispute resolution and toward efforts to help people solve their own disputes by talking them out with the help of a trained mediator. The idea is to get the parties to arrive at an agreement--usually a reasonable compromise--that seems fair to all. For more information on mediation, see The People's Law Review, which contains a lot of material on mediation and the many mediation projects around the United States (order information at the back of this book).

Unfortunately, at least as far as Small Claims Court is concerned, California lags behind in giving people the opportunity to mediate their disputes. Unlike New York City, for example, where everyone is offered an arbitration-mediation alternative to a court trial, mediation is currently available only in a few areas as isolated experiments. Where mediation is attempted, it is successful as much as 80% of the time.

7.

Who Can Sue?

In most situations, asking who can sue in Small
Claims Court is an easy question. You can as long as
you are eighteen years of age, have not been declared
mentally incompetent in a judicial proceeding and are
suing on your own claim.[1] Sometimes, however,
listing yourself as the party bringing suit isn't
quite so easy.

Here are the rules:

1. If you are suing for yourself alone, simply
list your full name where it says "Plaintiff" on the

---

1 Minors emancipated under Sections 60-70 of the California Civil
Code can also sue and be sued. This includes minors on active duty
with the military, married minors and minors emancipated by court
order. A prisoner can sue by either waiving a personal appearance
and submitting a written declaration to the court or by having
another person (other than a lawyer) appear on his/her behalf.
C.C.P. 117.4.

"Plaintiff's Statement" and sign the "declaration under penalty of perjury" on the "Claim of Plaintiff" form (see sample forms in Chapter 10).

2. If more than one person is bringing suit, list all the names on the "Plaintiff's Statement." Only one person need sign the "declaration under penalty of perjury" stating that all the information given is true and correct (see Chapter 10).

3. If you are filing a claim on behalf of an individually-owned business, the owner of the business must do the suing. He/she should list his/her name and the business name as plaintiffs on the "Plaintiff's Statement." The "declaration under penalty of perjury" should be signed in the business owner's name (see Chapter 10).

4. If you are filing a claim on behalf of a partnership, list the partnership name as plaintiff. Only one of the partners need sign the "declaration under penalty of perjury" (see Chapter 10).

5. If you are filing a claim on behalf of a corporation, whether profit or non-profit, list the corporation as plaintiff. The "declaration under penalty of perjury" must be signed by either:

a. an officer of the corporation

or

b. a person authorized to file claims on behalf of the corporation by the Board of Directors of the corporation.

If a non-officer of a corporation is involved, the court clerk will want to see some documentation

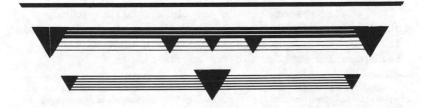

that the person suing is properly authorized. Here
is a sample authorization statement that you can use.

```
                    RESOLUTION - SMALL CLAIMS
                 APPOINTING A CORPORATION REPRESENTATIVE

       It appears to the Board of Directors of _____Acme Illusions, Inc._____

    _____,

    a corporation, qualified to do business in the State of California, that it is ne-

    cessary to appoint an agent for this corporation to act for and in its behalf in the

    Small Claims Court of ____Oakland-Piedmont_____Judicial District,

    County of_Alameda_____, State of California, that ___KEIJA SOTO_____

    is a suitable individual for such appointment.

       It is therefore resolved that ____KEIJA SOTO_____

    be and ___he is appointed to represent and appear for said corporation in the lawful

    process of any and all claims filed in the above named court, and ___he is further

    authorized to accept service of process issued by said court, for and on behalf of

    said corporation.

       I certify that foregoing resolution was adopted by the Board of Directors of this

    corporation, at a regular meeting of said board, held on ____(Date)_____ .

                                            Tom Jake
                                            Secretary

    (SEAL)
                                                Acme Illusions, Inc.
    The local business address of this corporation is:  100 Primrose Path
                                                Oakland, CA
        Keija Soto
    (Signature of agent so appointed)

     41 Mandrake, Oakland, CA.
    (Address of agent)
```

If you use a particular Small Claims Court regularly, you can often file a copy of the authorization
in its permanent file.[2]

     6. When a claim arises out of damage to a motor
vehicle, the registered owner(s) of the vehicle must
file in Small Claims Court. This means that, if you
are driving someone else's car and get hit by a third
party, you can't sue for damage done to the car. The
registered owner must do the suing.

     7. If you are suing on behalf of a public
entity such as a public library, city tax assessor's
office or county hospital, you must show the court
clerk proper authorization to sue.

---

2 Local rules differ as to requirements for filing on behalf of a
corporation. Some courts no longer require an authorization adopted
by the Board of Directors. Call your Small Claims clerk.

CONTRACTOR'S NOTE: Unlicensed contractors may not use any California court to collect money for a job for which a license was required even if they did excellent work. In Small Claims actions where the defendant does not raise this rule an unlicensed contractor may slip by, but don't count on it. (Business and Professions Code Section 7031.)

A. Participation by Attorneys

Attorneys, or other people acting as representatives, cannot normally appear in Small Claims Court. There are several exceptions to this rule. The major one allows attorneys to appear to sue or defend their own claims. Attorneys are also allowed to use Small Claims Court to sue or defend on behalf of a partnership when all other partners are also attorneys, and on behalf of a professional corporation of which the attorney is an officer or director and all other officers and directors are attorneys (C.C.P. 117.4).

B. Suits By Minors

If you are a minor (have not yet reached your eighteenth birthday), your parent or legal guardian must sue for you, unless you are emancipated under Sections 60-70 of the California Civil Code. To do this, a form must be filled out and signed by the judge appointing the person in question as your "Guardian Ad Litem." This simply means guardian for the purposes of the lawsuit. Ask the court clerk for a "Petition for Appointment of Guardian Ad Litem" form.

Here is a sample. It must be signed by both minor and guardian. When you have filled it out,

take it to the Small Claims Court clerk and arrange
to have the judge add his signature at the bottom,
under "ORDER."

```
. . . . . . . . . . . . . . . . . . . . . . . . . . . . COURT, SMALL CLAIMS DIVISION
. . . . . . . . . . . . . . . . . . . . . . . . . . . . . . . . . . . JUDICIAL DISTRICT
                    (Address and Telephone Number of Court)
. . . . . . . . . . . . . . . . . . . . . . . . . . . . . . . COUNTY, CALIFORNIA


        PLAINTIFF                           DEFENDANT(S)




        PETITION AND ORDER FOR APPOINTMENT OF GUARDIAN AD LITEM
                          PETITION

   I,_____

a minor, of the age of_____years and the _____
                                        (Plaintiff/Defendant)
in the above entitled cause, request that _____be
                                        (name of proposed guardian)
appointed guardian ad litem of the within named minor.
DATED:_____      _____
                                                (Petitioner)

                   CONSENT OF GUARDIAN

   I consent to my appointment as guardian ad litem for _____
                                                (name of minor)
in the above entitled cause and agree to serve in that capacity.
DATED:_____      _____
                                                 (Guardian)

                        ORDER

   It is ordered that the above petition be granted and that _____
                                                (name of guardian)
_____ be appointed guardian ad litem for and on behalf of the
above named minor in the above entitled cause.
DATED:_____      _____
                                        (Judge of the Municipal Court)
```

C. Class Actions

In Small Claims Court there is no such thing as a true class action lawsuit where a number of people in a similar situation join together in one lawsuit. However, a number of community groups have discovered that if a large number of people with a particular grievance (pollution, noise, etc.) sue the same defendant at the same time, something remarkably like a class action suit is created. This technique was pioneered by a stubborn group of homeowners near the San Francisco Airport who have several times won over 100 Small Claims Court judgments on the same day. They hired expert witnesses, did research, ran training workshops and hired lawyers when needed as part of a coordinated effort while all arguing their own cases. For more information on how they organized their effort, write to Nolo Press and ask for the Airport stories.

It used to be that the owners of small unincorporated businesses were discouraged from using Small Claims Court. This was because there was a legal requirement that stated that the owner of the business had to file the papers himself or herself and show up in court. For example, a dentist who wished to sue on an overdue bill would have to be in court personally. But California and a number of other states are more understanding of business time pressures and allow both incorporated and unincorporated businesses to send employees to court when the case involves unpaid bills. Thus, in California it would be proper for the dentist, dressmaker, or landlord to send the person who keeps the books to court when a bill isn't paid (C.C.P. 117.4). The person who goes to court must conform to the requirements of Section 1271 of the California Evidence Code which requires:

    a. The writing was made in the regular course of business;

    b. The writing was made at or near the time of the act, condition or event;

c. The custodian or other qualified witness
testifies to its identity and the mode of its preparation; and

d. The sources of information and method and
time of preparation were such as to indicate trustworthiness.

NOTE: California forbids the use of Small
Claims Court by collection agencies ("assignees")
suing on someone else's claim (C.C.P. 117.5).

8.

Who Can Be Sued?

You can sue almost anybody (person, partner-·
ship, corporation, government, etc.) in Small
Claims Court. Indeed, it is more often the "where
can I sue" problem (see Chapter 9), not the "who can
I sue" problem that causes difficulties. For example, you can sue David Rockefeller or the Chase
Manhattan Bank, but you will find it very difficult
to have the case heard in Sacramento, California, or
Emporia, Kansas, unless you can show that Rockefeller
or the bank lives or does business there, or entered
into or agreed to carry out a contract with you
there. This doesn't mean that you have a problem
with suing Rockefeller or the bank--you don't. The
problem is only with suing in Sacramento or Emporia.
If you go to New York where both Rockefeller and the
bank are located, you can bring your suit with no
problem.

Here are some hints that may prove helpful when it comes to filling out your papers. Again, the information I give here is based on California rules. You will want to check the forms set out in Chapter 10 B as you go along.

A. Suing One Person

If you are suing an individual, simply name him or her, using the most complete name that you have for that person. If the person calls himself J. R. Smith and you don't know what the J. stands for, simply sue him as J. R. Smith.

B. Suing Two Or More People

If you are suing more than one person on a claim arising from the same incident or contract, you must list and serve (see Chapter 11) each to properly bring them before the court. With a husband and wife, you must list each separately.

EXAMPLE: J. R. and June Smith, who are married, borrow $400 from you to start an avocado pit polishing business. Unfortunately, in the middle of the polishing, the seeds begin to sprout. J. R. and June get discouraged and refuse to pay you. If you wish to sue them and get a judgment, you should list them as J. R. Smith and June Smith--not Mr. and Mrs. Smith. But now suppose that J. R. borrowed $400 for the avocado pit business in January, June borrowed $500 to fix her motorcycle a month later and neither loan was repaid. In this situation, you would sue each in separate Small Claims actions.

C. Suing An Individually Owned Business

Here you list the name of the owner and the name of the business (i.e., J. R. Smith--doing business as [d.b.a.] Smith's Texaco). Don't assume that the name of the business is in fact the same as the name of the owner. Often it is not. Jim's Garage may be owned by Pablo Garcia Motors, Inc. (see Section E below). If you get a judgment against Jim's Garage and there is no Jim, you will find that it's worthless, unless you take steps to have the judgment changed to reflect the correct name under C.C.P. Section 117.19. This can take time and trouble so be sure you know who the owner of the business is before you sue.

California requires that all people doing business in a name other than their own file a Fictitious Business Name Statement with the county clerk in the county or counties in which the business operates. This is public information and you can get it from the court clerk. Another way to figure out who owns a business is to check with the Business Tax and License Office in the city where the business is located. If the business is not in an incorporated area, try the county. The tax and license office will have a list of the owners of all businesses paying taxes in the city. They should be able to tell you, for example, that the Garden of Exotic Delights is owned by Rufus Clod. Once you find this out, you sue Rufus Clod, d.b.a. The Garden of Exotic Delights.

If for some reason the tax and license office and the county clerk can't help, you may want to check with the state. Millions of people, from exterminators to embalmers, must register with one or another office in Sacramento. So, if your beef is with a teacher, architect, smog control device installer, holder of a beer or wine license, etc., you will very likely be able to learn who and where they are with a letter or phone call. Check the Sacramento County phone book under "California."

NOTE: If you do sue the owner of a business using a fictitious name under an incorrect name, C.C.P. Section 117.19 allows you to substitute the correct name either at the court hearing or after judgment. Ask the Small Claims Court clerk for more information.

D. Suing Partnerships

List the names of all the business partners even if your dispute is only with one (Patricia Sun and Farah Moon, d.b.a. Sacramento Gardens). See Section C just above for information on how to learn just who owns what. Never assume that you know who owns a business without checking. All partners to a business are individually liable for all the acts of the business.

EXAMPLE: You go to a local cleaners with your new, sky blue suit. They put too much cleaning fluid on it with the result that a small grey cloud settles on the rear right shoulder. After unsuccessfully trying to get the cleaners to take responsibility for improving the weather on the back of your suit, you start thinking about a different kind of suit. When you start filling out your court papers (see Chapter 10), you realize that you know only that the stores says "Perfection Cleaners" on the front and that the guy who has been so unpleasant to you is named Bob. You call the city business tax and license people and they tell you that Perfection Cleaners is owned by Robert Johnson and Sal De Benno. You should sue both and also list the name of the business.

NOTE: It is wise to get a judgment against more than one person if possible. When it comes to trying to collect, it's always nice to have someone in reserve if one defendant turns out to be an artful dodger.

E. Suing A Corporation

Corporations are legal people. This means that you can sue, and enforce a judgment against, a corporation itself. You should not sue the owners of the corporation or its officers or managers as individuals unless you have a personal claim against them that is separate from their role as part of the corporation. In most situations the real people who own or operate the corporation aren't themselves liable to pay for the corporation's debts. This is called "limited liability" and is part of the reason that many people choose to incorporate.

Be sure to list the full name of the corporation when you file suit (John's Liquors, Inc., a Corporation). Here again, the name on the door or the stationery may not be the real name. Corporations too sometimes do business using fictitious names. Check with the city or county business license people where the corporation does business. In addition, the California Secretary of State's office, Corporate Status Unit, 1230 J Street, Sacramento, California a 95814 maintains a complete list of all California corporations, and all out-of-state corporations "qualified" to do business in California. You may sue a corporation with headquarters in another state in California as long as they do business here.

F. Suing On A Motor Vehicle Accident

Here there are some special rules. If your claim arises from an accident with an automobile, motorcycle, truck or R.V., you should name both the driver of the vehicle and the registered owner as part of your suit.[1] Most times you will have gotten this information at the time of the accident. If a police accident report was made, it will also contain this information. You can get a copy of any police report from the police department for a modest fee. If there was no police report, contact the Department of Motor Vehicles. For a small fee, they will tell you who owns any vehicle for which you have a license number.[2]

---

1 This is the general common sense rule, not a legal requirement. In a rare situation (one person has died, or is out of the state or country) you may wish to proceed against the other person alone.

2 The D.M.V. will ask you why you want this information. Simply tell them "to file a lawsuit based on a motor vehicle accident." This is a legitimate reason and you will get the information you need. The owner of the car will, however, be notified of your request.

Remember, when you sue more than one person (in this case the driver and the owner if they are different), you serve papers on both. When a business owns a vehicle, sue both the driver and the owners of the business.

G. Special Procedures For Suits Against Minors

It is very difficult to sue a minor for breach of contract because minors can disavow (back out of) any contract they sign as long as they do it before they turn eighteen, unless the contract was for a necessity of life, i.e., food, in which case the parents are responsible.[3] You can sue minors for damage to your person or property. If you wish to do so, you must also list a parent or legal guardian on the court papers. You could do it like this:

"John Jefferey, a minor, and William Jefferey, his father."

It is very difficult to collect from minors themselves as most don't have money or income. Of course, there are exceptions to this rule, but most minors are, almost by definition, broke. Thus, it doesn't usually pay to bother with suits against minors unless you can collect from the minor's parents. Normally a parent is not legally responsible to pay for damages by his or her children. However, when a child is guilty of "willful misconduct," a parent can be liable up to $5,000 per act ($30,000 if a gun is involved). Parents are also liable for damage done by their minor children in auto accidents when they authorized the child to drive.

3 Any exception to this general rule that minors can disavow their contracts has to do with minors emancipated under Civil Code Sections 60-70. Minors who are on active duty in the armed services, are legally married or who have been emancipated by court order must stand behind their contracts as if they were adults.

EXAMPLE 1: John Johnson, age 17, trips over his shoelace while delivering your newspaper and crashes through your glass door. Can you recover from John's parents? Probably not, as John is not guilty of "willful misconduct."

EXAMPLE 2: John shoots out the same glass door with a slingshot after you have repeatedly asked his parents to disarm him. Can you recover from the parents? Probably.

H. Special Rules For Suits Against Government Agencies

In California before you can sue a city because your car was illegally towed away or a city employee caused you damage, or for any other reason involving personal injury or property damage, you must first file a claim with the city and have it denied. Get a claim form from the city clerk. Your claim must be filed within 100 days of the date of the incident. The city attorney will review your claim and make a recommendation to the City Council. Sometimes the recommendation will be to pay you--most often it will be to deny your claim. Once the City Council acts, you will receive a letter. If it's a denial, take it with you when you file your Small Claims action. The clerk will want to see it.

The rules for suits against counties are basically the same. Get your complaint form from the clerk of the Board of Supervisors. Complete and file it within 100 days of the incident. Within a month or so after filing, you will be told whether your claim is approved or denied. If your claim is denied, you can then proceed to file in Small Claims Court.

Claims against the State of California must also be filed within 100 days for personal injury and property damage. Claims should be filed with the State Board of Control, Suite 300, 926 J Street, Sacramento, California 95814.

Suits against the federal government, a federal agency, or even against a federal employee for actions relating to his or her employment should probably not be brought in Small Claims Court. Government lawyers routinely have such cases transferred to a federal district court (perhaps hundreds of miles away) where lawyers and formal procedures are the norm. Unfortunately, there is no federal Small Claims procedure.

I. Suing Contractors And Their Bonding Companies

Whenever you sue a contractor for anything relating to work s/he had done improperly (or not at all), you may find that s/he is "bonded" by a "surety" or "guaranty" company. You can sue and collect a judgment from this kind of company, based on the contractor's poor workmanship or failure to abide by the agreement. However, to do this you must also sue the contractor and succeed in serving your papers on him/her (see Chapter 11). If you don't sue the contractor, or even if you do but can't serve your papers on him or her (perhaps because s/he has skipped town), your case against the surety company will be transferred to the formal court system where, again, lawyers and formal procedure are the norm (C.C.P. 117.6).

9.

Where Can I Sue?

Small Claims Courts are local. This makes sense because the amounts involved aren't large enough to make it worthwhile to require people to travel great distances. A Small Claims Court judicial district covers an individual city, several cities, or a county. The next city or county will have its own similar, but separate, Small Claims Court. Normally, your dispute will be with a person or business located nearby. You can sue in the judicial district where the defendant resides or, if a corporation is involved, where its main place of business is located. Sometimes though, it is not so easy to understand where to file your suit. This might be the case if the person you wish to sue lives 100 (or 500) miles away, or has moved since the dispute arose. As long as the person you want to sue lives in California, or does business here, however, you can bring suit in Small Claims Court in California.

If the person you want to sue has no contact with California, however, you almost surely can't sue here, but must sue in the state where the defendant is located.

On the first page of the first chapter we asked you to get a copy of the rules for your local Small Claims Court.[1] Refer to them now. The first thing you will wish to understand are the geographical boundaries of the Small Claims Court judicial district. If this information is not set out in the information sheet, call the clerk of the court and ask. You may be able to sue in more than one judicial district. If this is the case, choose the one that is most convenient to you.

Summary Of California Rules As To Where You Can Sue

You can sue in any judicial districts where:

   A. The defendant resides;

   B. A corporate defendant does business;

   C. Injury to persons or personal property occurred;

   D. Defendant entered into a contract (does not apply to retail installment or to auto sales contracts);

   E. An obligation (contract) was to be performed (does not apply to retail installment or auto sales contracts or those to furnish goods, services, or loans intended for personal or household use);

---

1 Small Claims Court is usually held on a weeekday, often at 8:30 or 9:00 A.M. All larger areas must also provide for either Saturday or evening sessions.

F.   At the time the contract was entered into the defendant resided or a corporate defendant did business (does not apply to a retail installment or auto finance sale).

Special Rules for Retail Installment Contracts

On a retail installment contract you can sue in the judicial district where:

G.   The buyer signed the contract;

H.   The buyer resided at the time the contract was signed;

I.   The buyer resides at time of suit;

J.   Goods are attached to real property.

Special Rules for Autos Subject to the Automobile Sales Finance Act:

On an auto purchase contract you can sue in the judicial district where:

K.   The buyer signed the contract;

L.   The buyer resided at the time the contract was signed;

M.   The vehicle is permanently garaged.

NOTE: As a general rule, it is not possible to bring a person who lives or does business in another state or country into a California Small Claims Court.   However, if an out-of-state business sells its products in California you can sue them here and serve the court papers on the business where they are located.

Now let's look at the rules as to where you can sue in more detail:

A. You Can Sue A Person Where He Resides/Or a Corporation Where It Does Business

This rule makes good sense, doesn't it? If a suit is brought where the defendant is located, he or she can't complain that it is unduly burdensome to appear. Books have been written about the technical definition of residence. Indeed, I remember with horror trying to sort out a law school exam in which the professor had given a person with numerous homes and businesses "contact" with six different judicial districts. The point of the examination was for us students to figure out where he could be sued. Thankfully, you don't have to worry about this sort of nonsense. If you believe a business or individual to be sufficiently present within a particular judicial district so that it would not be a hardship for them to appear in court there, go ahead and file your suit. The worst that can happen--and this is highly unlikely--is that the judge or clerk will tell you to start over someplace else or transfer your case to another judicial district.

EXAMPLE: Downhill Skier lives in the city, but also owns a mountain cabin where he spends several months a year. Late one snowy afternoon, Downhill drives his new Porsche from the ski slopes to his ultra-modern, rustic cabin. Turning into his driveway, he skids and does a bad slalom turn right into Woodsey Carpenter's 1957 International Harvester Pickup. Where can Woodsey sue? He can sue in the city where Downhill has his permanent address. He can probably also sue in the county where the cabin is located, on the theory that Downhill also lives there. But read on--as you will see under Section C below, it isn't necessary for Woodsey to even get into the residence question, as he can also sue in the mountain county on the theory that the injury occurred there.

NOTE: You can sue multiple defendants in any judicial district in which one resides even though the other(s) live in another part of the state.

B. The Contract Which Is The Basis Of Your Suit Was Signed In A Particular Judicial District

In addition to suing where the defendant resides, you can also sue at the place where an obligation (contract) was signed. This, too, is good common sense as the law assumes that, if people contract at a certain location, it is probably reasonably convenient to both. If, for example, Downhill gets a telephone installed in his cabin, or has the fender on his Porsche fixed, or has a cesspool put in, or agrees to sit for a portrait in the mountain county, he can be sued there if he fails to keep his part of the bargain. Of course, as we learned above, Downhill might also be sued in the city where he resides permanently.

EXAMPLE: John Gravenstein lives in Sonoma County, California, where he owns an apple orchard. He signs a contract with Acme Mechanical Apple Picker Co., an international corporation with offices in San Francisco, New York, Paris and Guatemala City. John signs the contract in Sonoma County. The parts are sent to John from San Francisco via U.P.S. They turn out to be defective. After trying and failing to reach a settlement with Acme, John wants to know if he can sue them in Sonoma County. Yes. Even though Acme doesn't have a business office in Sonoma County and they performed no action there in connection with their agreement to sell John the spare parts, the contract was signed there.

REMINDER: You should now realize that there are often several reasons why it can be O.K. to bring a suit in a particular place. You only need one, but it never hurts to have several. Also, as you should now understand, there may be two, three or more judicial districts in which you can file your case. In this situation, simply choose the one most convenient to you. If you choose the wrong one your action will be transferred.

CONTRACT NOTE: It isn't always easy to know where a contract has been "entered into" (see (C) under the Summary above) in a situation where the people making the contract are at different locations. If you enter a contract over the phone, for example, there could be an argument that the contract was entered into either where you are or where the other party is.[2] Rather than trying to learn all the intricacies of contract law, your best bet is probably to sue in the place most convenient to you. On the other hand, if someone sues you at the wrong end of the state and you believe they have not met any of the requirements set out in the Summary above, write the court as soon as you are served and ask that the case be transferred to a court closer to you. Either way, if in doubt let the judge decide.

C. An Injury To A Person Or To His/Her Property Occurred Within A Particular Judicial District

This means, quite simply, that, if you are in a car accident, a dog bites you, a tree falls on your noggin, or a neighbor floods your cactus garden, etc., you can sue in the judicial district where the injury occurred.

EXAMPLE: Downhill is returning to his home in San Francisco. He is driving his Porsche carefully, still thankful that no one was injured when he hit Woodsey. At the same time, John Gravenstein is rushing to the city to try and get spare parts for his still broken apple picker. John jumps a red light and crumples Downhill's other fender. The accident occurs in Marin County, a county in which neither John nor Downhill live. After parking his car and taking a taxi home, Downhill tries to figure out where he can sue if he can't work out a fair

---

2 To vastly oversimplify, a contract needs both an offer and an acceptance to exist. If I call you and order two widgets and you say O.K., the contract was probably entered into at your location. However, if you write me and order the widgets and I file the order, the contract very likely was entered into where I am.

settlement with John.   Unfortunately for him, he can't sue in San Francisco as John doesn't reside there and the accident occurred in Marin.   Downhill would have to sue either in Marin County, where his property was damaged, or in Sonoma County, where John lives.   Luckily for Downhill, Marin County adjoins San Francisco.   Had the accident occurred in Los Angeles County, however, Downhill would have been put to a lot more trouble if he wished to sue.

D. Special Rules For Retail Installment Sales Contracts And Motor Vehicles Finance Sales

If your case involves a motor vehicle or a major piece of property such as a television or appliance that you bought on time, you may file suit where you presently live, where the vehicle or goods are permanently kept, where you lived when you entered into the contract or where you signed the contract.

EXAMPLE: Downhill buys a major appliance on time subject to the Retail Installment Sales Act while he lives in San Francisco.   Later he moves to Fresno and stops paying his bill.   Can he be sued for the unpaid balance in San Francisco?   Yes.

10.

Plaintiff's and Defendant's Filing Fees, Court Papers and Court Dates

A. How Much Does It Cost?

For people who have filed 12 or fewer claims in any given court over the past 12 months, the Small Claims filing fee in California is $6.00, both for filing a "Claim of Plaintiff" and a "Claim of Defendant." For more frequent filers, the fee is $12.00.[1] There is an additional $3.00 fee for serving papers by certified mail on each defendant. You can recover your filing and service costs if you win (see Chapter 15).

B. Filling Out Your Court Papers And Getting Your Court Date

Now let's look at the initial court papers themselves to be sure that you don't trip over a detail. Forms in use in California are all substantially the same although there are differences in detail in the different judicial districts. You should have little trouble filling out your papers by following the examples printed here but, if you do, simply ask the clerk for help. Small Claims clerks are required by law to give you as much help as possible short of practicing law (whatever that is). A friendly, courteous approach to the clerk can often result in much helpful information and advice.

---

1 C.C.P. Section 117.14.

Step 1 "The Plaintiff's Statement"

To start your case in Small Claims Court, go to the Small Claims clerk's office and fill out the form entitled "Plaintiff's Statement." If you have carefully read the first nine chapters of this book, this should be easy. Be particularly careful that you are suing in the right judicial district (Chapter 9) and that you are properly naming the defendant (Chapter 8).

Alameda County Municipal _____ COURT, SMALL CLAIMS DIVISION

Oakland - Piedmont _____ JUDICIAL DISTRICT

600 Washington St.

(Address and Telephone Number of Court)

Oakland - Alameda _____ COUNTY, CALIFORNIA

PLAINTIFF'S STATEMENT

How to Designate Parties in a Small Claims Action

INDIVIDUAL –
    "John L. Doe"
    Individual named as plaintiff must sign claim.

HUSBAND AND WIFE –
    "James A. Smith and Mary Smith"
    Either husband or wife may sign claim.

INDIVIDUAL DOING BUSINESS UNDER A FICTITIOUS FIRM NAME –
    "John Doe, doing business as Acme Sign Service"
    Owner must sign claim.

MINOR REPRESENTED BY GUARDIAN AD LITEM –
    "James Doe, a minor, by John Doe, his guardian ad litem"
    Guardian must sign claim. Petition and Order must be filed.

PARTNERSHIP –
    "John Doe and Richard Doe, a co-partnership"
    Any partner may sign claim.

CORPORATION –
    "ABC Industries, a corporation"
    Officer of corporation, member of board of directors, or authorized person must sign claim.

UNINCORPORATED ASSOCIATION –
    "M. N. Society, by John Doe, as president (or other officer)"
    Officer representing association must sign claim.

1. State your name and residence address, and the name and address of any other person joining with you in this action. If this claim arises from a business transaction, give the name and address of your business.

    Name Andrew Printer
    a.
    Address 1800 Marilee St., Fremont, CA _____ Phone No. 827-7000

    Name
    b.
    Address _____ Phone No. _____

2. State the name and address of each person or business firm you are suing; If this claim arises from an automobile accident, you must give the name and address of both the driver and registered owner.

    Name Acme Illusions, Inc.
    a.
    Address 100 Primrose Path, Oakland, CA

    Name
    b.
    Address

    Name
    c.
    Address

(Continued on Reverse Side)

Step 2 "The Claim Of Plaintiff"

When you have completed your "Plaintiff's Statement," give it to the county clerk who will then use it to type out your "Claim of Plaintiff" form and assign your case a number. All parties bringing suit will be asked to sign this form under penalty of perjury. A copy of the "Claim of Plaintiff" will go to the judge and another must be served on the defendant (see Chapter 11). Here is a sample of the "Claim of Plaintiff."

Alameda County Municipal .... COURT, SMALL CLAIMS DIVISION
Oakland-Piedmont .... JUDICIAL DISTRICT
600 Washington St. ___(Address and Telephone Number of Court)___

Oakland - Alameda .... COUNTY, CALIFORNIA

NO S C _____

PLAINTIFF (Name and address)	DEFENDANT (Name and address of each)
Andrew Printer 1800 Marilee Street Fremont, California 94536	Acme Illusions, Inc. 100 Primrose Path Oakland, California 94602

**CLAIM OF PLAINTIFF
AND ORDER**

CLAIM OF PLAINTIFF

1. Defendant is indebted to plaintiff in the sum of $ 600.00 .... not including court costs, for failure to pay for printing and typesetting

2. Plaintiff has demanded that defendant pay this sum and it has not been paid

3. This court is the proper court for the hearing because
   a. [X] At least one defendant now resides or a corporate defendant does business in this judicial district.
   b. [ ] Injury to person or damage to personal property occurred in this judicial district.
   c. [X] Defendant entered into or signed in this judicial district a contract not involving a retail installment account or an auto finance sale.
   d. [ ] The obligation was to be performed in this judicial district on a contract not involving a retail installment account, an auto finance sale, or the furnishing of goods, services, or loans intended primarily for personal, family, or household use.
   e. [ ] Defendant resided or a corporate defendant did business in this judicial district at the time the contract was entered into for the furnishing of goods, services or loans intended primarily for personal, family, or household use, and not involving a retail installment account or an auto finance sale.
   f. [ ] This action is on a retail installment account or contract (CC 1812.10), specify
   g. [ ] This action is on a motor vehicle finance sale (CC 2984.4), specify

4. I understand that
   a. Although I may consult an attorney. I cannot be represented by an attorney at the trial in the small claims division
   b. I must appear at the time and place for trial and have with me witnesses and evidence (Such as books, papers, receipts, and exhibits) to prove my claim.
   c. I have no right of appeal from a judgment on my claim.
   I declare (Certify) under penalty of perjury that the foregoing is true and correct and that this declaration is executed
   on (Date) (fill in date) at (Place) .Fremont. , California

   Andrew Printer
   Signature of declarant

(Continued on reverse side)

The declaration under penalty of perjury must be signed in California or in a state that authorizes use of a declaration in place of an affidavit. Otherwise an affidavit is required

Form Approved by the
Judicial Council of California
Effective January 1, 1977

**CLAIM OF PLAINTIFF
AND ORDER**

CCP 116.2, 116.4, 116.6, 117.1

Step 3 Getting A Hearing Date

One of the great advantages of Small Claims Court is that disputes are settled quickly. This is important. Many people avoid lawyers and the regular courts primarily because they take forever to get a dispute settled. Business people, for example, increasingly rely on private arbitration, caring more that a dispute be resolved promptly than that they win a complete victory. Anyone who has had to wait for two years for a case to be heard in some constipated state trial court knows through bitter experience that the old cliche, "justice delayed is justice denied," is all too true.

In California, Section 116.4(b) of the Code of Civil Procedure requires that, if the defendant resides in the same county in which the action is brought, the hearing should be no sooner than 10 days, or longer than 40 days from the time the papers are filed. If the defendant lives outside of the county where you bring suit, the case will be heard not less than 30, nor more than 70 days from the date you file your complaint. If there is more than one defendant, and one or more lives in the county where you file and one or more in another county, the case will be treated as if all defendants live within your county: that is, the case will be heard within 30 days of the time the papers are filed.

When you file your papers, you should also arrange with the clerk for a court date. Get a date that is convenient for you. You need not take the first date the clerk suggests. Be sure to leave yourself enough time to get a copy of the "Claim of Plaintiff" form served on the defendant(s). (See Chapter 11 for service information.) If you fail to properly serve your papers on the defendant in time, there is no big hassle--just notify the clerk, get a new court date, and try again.

Small Claims Courts are most often held at 9:00 A.M. on work days. Larger counties are required to hold at least one evening or Saturday session per month. Ask the clerk for a schedule.

Filing Your Papers By Mail: It is possible to file papers by mail in Small Claims Court. I recommend it only if you are a long distance from the court you must sue in (see Chapter 9 - Where Can I Sue?). Send double first class postage to the court clerk with your request. They will return the Plaintiff's Statement and Claim of Plaintiff. Fill out the former and sign the latter. Return both to the clerk with your filing fee and money for certified mail service if you wish to follow this service approach. The details of all this can get confusing. After you get your packet of forms you will probably want to call the clerk to review them.

C. The Defendant's Forms

No papers need be filed to defend a case in Small Claims Court. You just show up on the date and at the time indicated, ready to tell your side of the story. If you need to get the hearing delayed, see Section D below. It is proper, and advisable, for a defendant to call or write the plaintiff and see if a fair settlement can be reached without going to court (see Chapter 6).

Sometimes someone sues you in a situation where you were planning to sue them (i.e., a traffic accident where you each believe the other is at fault). As long as your grievance stems from the same incident, you can file a "Claim of Defendant" for up to $1,500 in Small Claims Court and have it heard by a judge at the same time that the plaintiff's claim against you is considered.[2] However, if you believe that the plaintiff owes you money as the result of a different injury or breach of contract, you must file your own separate case.

But what happens if you wish to make a claim against the plaintiff for more than $1,500? First

---

2 When you file a "Claim of Defendant," you become a plaintiff as far as this claim is concerned. This means that, if you lose, you can't appeal because plaintiffs can't appeal. Of course, if you lose on the original plaintiff's claim, you can appeal that portion of the judgment (see Chapter 22).

re-read Chapter 4 and decide whether you want to
scale down your claim to fit into Small Claims. If
you don't you must file your claim in either justice
or Municipal Court (up to $15,000) or Superior Court
(over $15,000) and pay all necessary filing fees.
Your next step is to file an affidavit setting forth
the facts of the higher court action with the Small
Claims Court clerk. This must be done prior to the
hearing date for the Small Claims Court case and
costs $1.00. In addition, a copy of this affidavit
must be delivered to the plaintiff in person. Now
it's up to the judge.

...Alameda County Municipal.............................COURT, SMALL CLAIMS DIVISION
...Oakland-Piedmont.......................................JUDICIAL DISTRICT
...600 Washington St.......................................
            (Address and Telephone Number of Court)

PLAINTIFF	DEFENDANT(S)
Andrew Printer 1800 Marilee St. Fremont, California 94536	Acme Illusions, Inc. 100 Primrose Path Oakland, California 94602

CLAIM OF DEFENDANT

HEARING SET IN THE ABOVE COURT ON_____at_____.

1. Plaintiff is indebted to defendant (name): __Acme Illusions, Inc.__
   in the sum of $__300.00____, not including court costs, for__delays and__
   __poor workmanship in printing job_____

2. Defendant has demanded that plaintiff pay this sum and it has not been paid.

3. I UNDERSTAND THAT:

   a. Although I may consult an attorney, I cannot be represented by an attorney
      at the trial in the Small Claims Division;

   b. I HAVE NO RIGHT OF APPEAL FROM A JUDGMENT ON MY CLAIM.

I declare (certify) under penalty of perjury that the foregoing is true and correct
and that this declaration is executed on,

(Date)_(fill in date)___ at (Place)_____Oakland_____, California.

Waldo Fergus President
            (Signature of Declarant)

_____
            (Telephone Number)

The declaration under penalty of perjury must be signed in California, or in a State
that authorizes use of a declaration in place of an affidavit; otherwise an affidavit
is required.

CLAIM OF DEFENDANT

Section 116.8 of the Code of Civil Procedure states:

"The Small Claims Court shall not transfer the
Small Claims Court action to the court set forth
in the affidavit until a judgment is rendered in
the Small Claims Court action, unless the ends
of justice would be served by such a prejudgment
transfer of the proceedings . . . . If the Small
Claims matter is transferred prior to judgment,
both actions shall be tried together in the
transferred court."

NOTE: If you have a claim against a plaintiff
for an amount less than the Small Claims Court maximum which arises out of the same transaction or situation that forms the basis of his or her suit against
you, you should file it prior to the time that the
plaintiff's case is heard. If you fail to file and
let the case be decided, you will have a tougher time
convincing the judge of the merits of your case later
on.

D. Changing A Court Date

It is sometimes impossible for a defendant to be
present on the day ordered by the court for the
hearing. It can also happen that the plaintiff will
pick out a court date and get the defendant served
only to find that an unexpected emergency makes it
impossible for him or her to be present.

It is normally not difficult to get a case
delayed. To arrange this, call the other party and
see if you can agree on a mutually convenient date.
Don't call the clerk first--they don't know what days
the other party has free. Sometimes it is difficult
to face talking to someone who you are involved in a
lawsuit with, but you will just have to swallow your
pride and start dialing. Once all parties have
agreed to a new date, notify the court clerk in
writing with the signatures of both parties. Here is
a sample:

```
                                        11 South Street
                                        San Diego, CA
                                        January 10, 19___

Clerk of the Small Claims Court
San Diego, California
                                        Re: SC 4117 Rodriguez v. McNally
Dear Clerk:

Mr. Rodriguez and I agree to request that you postpone this case to a
date after March 1, 19___.



                                        _____
                                        JOHN McNALLY


                                        _____
                                        JOHN RODRIGUEZ
```

If you speak to the other party(ies) and find that he or she is completely uncooperative, put your request for a delay (continuance) in writing, along with the circumstances that make it impossible for you to keep the first date. Send your letter to the judge of the Small Claims Court. Here is a sample:

```
                                        37 Birdwalk Blvd.
                                        Occidental, Calif.

                                        January 10, 19___

Judge John Justice
Small Claims Court
City Hall
San Francisco, Calif.          Re: Small Claims No. 374-628

Dear Judge Justice:

    I have been served with a complaint (No. 374-628) by John's Laundry,
Inc.  The date set for a hearing, February 15, falls on the day of my
son's graduation from Nursing School in Oscaloosa, Oklahoma, which my
husband and I plan to attend.

    I called John's Laundry and asked to have the case delayed one week.
They just laughed and said that they would not give me any cooperation.

    I feel that I have a good defense to this suit.  Please delay this
case until any day after February 22, except March 13, which is my day
for a medical check-up.


                                        Thank you,


                                        Sally Wren
```

E. If One Party Doesn't Show Up

If one party to a case doesn't appear in court on the proper day at the proper time, the case is normally decided in favor of the other. Depending on whether it is the plaintiff or defendant who fails to show up, the terms used by the judge to make his decision are different. If the plaintiff appears, but the defendant doesn't, a "default judgment" is normally entered in favor of the plaintiff (see Chapters 12 and 15 for more information on defaults). Occasionally, although it happens far less frequently, it is the plaintiff who fails to show up. In this situation, the judge may dismiss the case or decide it on the basis of the defendant's evidence. The defendant will usually prefer this result, especially if a Claim of Defendant has been made.

Unfortunately, if the case is dismissed "without prejudice" the plaintiff can bring it again.

1. Setting Aside A Default (Defendant's Remedy)

Courts are not very sympathetic to setting aside or vacating a default judgment to allow a defense to be made unless you can show that the original papers weren't properly served on you and that you didn't know about the hearing. This can happen if someone signs your name for the certified letter and then doesn't give it to you, or because a dishonest process server doesn't serve you, but tells the court he did, or for some other reason. As soon as you find out that a default judgment has been entered against you, call the court clerk. It doesn't make any difference if the hearing you missed was months before as long as you move to set it aside immediately upon learning about it.

If you have had a default judgment entered against you after you were properly served, you will face an uphill struggle to get it set aside. Some judges will accept excuses such as "I forgot," "I was sick," "I got called out of town," etc., and some

will not. Generally, judges assume that you could
have at least called, or had a friend call, no matter
what the emergency. However, if you act promptly
(this means within 30 days after the default), and if
you have a good excuse, you stand a reasonable chance
of getting the judge to set the default aside[3]
(C.C.P. 117.8(b)).

NOTE: You can't appeal from a default judgment
even if you have a great case. You must try to get
the default set aside or the judgment will be final.
To try to set aside a default, go to the Small Claims
clerk's office and ask for the proper form. This
must then be served on the plaintiff. If the Small

3 If the defendant was not properly served and did not appear at the
hearing in the Small Claims Court, the defendant has 180 days to move
to vacate after he or she discovers or should have discovered the
judgment was entered against him or her. C.C.P. Section 117.8(d).

Claims Court denies your motion to vacate the judgment after you have appeared in court or submitted a written justification, you may appeal as to this denial.

_____ COUNTY, CALIFORNIA
.....................Fill.in......................................COURT, SMALL CLAIMS DIVISION
....JUDICIAL DISTRICT

....
(Address and Telephone Number of Court)

| PLAINTIFF | DEFENDANT(S) |
| Andrew Printer | Acme Illusions, Inc. |

**NOTICE OF MOTION TO VACATE JUDGMENT
AND DECLARATION**

NOTICE OF MOTION TO VACATE JUDGMENT

1 To (Name) Acme Illusions, Inc.

2. A hearing will be held in the above-named court at which I will ask the court to set aside the judgment entered against me in this case. If you wish to oppose the motion you should appear at the court on

(Date)   at (Time)

3. This motion will be made on the grounds set forth below and will be based on this notice of motion and declaration, the records on file with the court, and any oral and documentary evidence that may be presented at the hearing.

DECLARATION FOR MOTION TO VACATE JUDGMENT

4. Judgment was entered against me in the above-entitled case on (Date)

5. This motion to vacate the judgment entered against me in this case is made on the following ground (reason)
   (a) [X] I was not properly served with the claim. I first learned of the entry of judgment against me
   on (Date) . . . . as follows (Specify facts)

      I received a notice of the judgement in the mail.

   (or)
   (b) [X] Other (Specify facts): A death in the family made it impossible to be present
                                   at the trial

I declare under penalty of perjury that the foregoing is true and correct and that this declaration is executed on
(Date): . . . . at (Place): . . . ., California.

Waldo Fergus, Pres., Acme Illusions, Inc.
            (Type or print name)   (Signature)

The declaration under penalty of perjury must be signed in California, or in a state that authorizes use of a declaration in place of an affidavit, otherwise an affidavit is required. A COPY OF THIS NOTICE MUST BE SERVED ON THE PERSON NAMED IN ITEM ONE

Form approved by the   **NOTICE OF MOTION TO VACATE JUDGMENT**   CCP 117.8
Judicial Council of California   **AND DECLARATION**   CCP 657
Effective January 1 1979

COLLECTION NOTE: After a default judgment has been entered, the plaintiff can begin collection activities immediately. There is no need to wait for the 20-day appeal period to end as the defendant has no right of appeal until the default is set aside. Therefore, a defendant who is vulnerable to a wage attachment or other immediate collection technique will need to file a "stay of execution" as well as a motion to set aside the default if a "writ of execution" has been issued (see Chapter 24). The stay of execution must be delivered to the same sheriff or marshal who has the writ of execution.

2. Vacating A Judgement of Dismissal (Plaintiff's Remedy)

Vacating a judgment of dismissal is only difficult if the dismissal is made "with prejudice to the suit being filed again." In the situation of an ordinary dismissal the plaintiff can simply refile the case. Why is it difficult for the plaintiff to get a dismissal entered "with prejudice" set aside? Because the plaintiff is the one who started the case and arranged for the court date. The judge assumes that the plaintiff should be able to show up for his or her own case, or at least, call the court clerk prior to the court date and explain why he or she can't appear.

However, now and then emergencies happen, or someone simply makes a mistake about the day. Judges can, and do, vacate dismissals "with prejudice" if both the following circumstances exist. One, the plaintiff moves to have the judgment vacated "immediately" upon learning of his mistake. "Immediately" never is interpreted to be more than 30 days from the date the dismissal is entered and is thought by most judges to be a much shorter time. Two, the plaintiff has a good explanation as to why he was unable to be present or call on the day the case was regularly scheduled. A judge might accept something like this: "I had a flu with a high fever and simply lost track of a couple of days. As soon as I felt better, which was two days after my case was dismissed, I came to the clerk's office to try to get this case rescheduled."

To get a judgment "with prejudice" vacated, you must fill out the same form as the one set out in Section 1.

11.

Serving Your Papers

After you have filed your "Claim of Plaintiff" form with the clerk following the instructions in Chapter 10 B, a copy must be served on the person, persons, or corporation you are suing. This is called "service of process." Your lawsuit is not complete without it. The reason that you must serve the other side is simple--the person(s) you are suing are entitled to be notified of the general nature of your claim and the day, time and place when they can show up to defend themselves.

A. Who Must Be Served

All defendants that you list on your "Claim of Plaintiff" should be served. It is not enough to serve one defendant and assume that he or she will tell the other(s). This is true even if the defendants are married, or living together. If you don't serve a particular defendant, the court can't enter a judgment against that person. If you sue more than one person and can serve only one, a judge can enter a judgment against the person served, in effect dropping your action against the other defendant(s).

B. How To Serve Your Papers

There are several approved ways to serve papers. All depend on your knowing where the defendant is. If you can't find the defendant, you can't serve him and it makes little sense to file a lawsuit.

Method 1   Personal Service:

Any person who is eighteen years of age, or older, except the person bringing the suit, may serve the defendant by handing him the "Claim of Plaintiff" anyplace in California.[1] Any person means just that--you can hire the county sheriff or marshal (often good for its sobering effect), or a private process server (listed in the Yellow Pages), or you can have a friend or relative do the service. Only you can't serve the papers in your lawsuit.

The "Claim of Plaintiff" must be handed to the defendant personally. You can't simply leave the paper at his or her job, or home, or in the mailbox. A person making a service who doesn't know the person involved should make sure that he or she is serving the right person. If a defendant refuses to take the paper, acts hostile or attempts to run away, the process server should simply put the paper down and leave. Valid service has been accomplished. The process server should never try to use force to get a defendant to take any papers.

---

1 Small Claims papers cannot validly be served out-of-state (C.C.P. Section 116.4).

Method 2 By Certified Mail:

You can also serve your "Claim of Plaintiff" by
certified mail. The clerk of the court does the
mailing for you. The fee in California is $3.00 for
each defendant. This is recoverable if you win (see
Chapter 15 C). The mail method is both cheap and
easy, but it depends for its success on the defendant
signing for the letter. Most businesses and many
individuals routinely sign to accept mail. However,
some people never do, knowing instinctively, or perhaps from past experience, that nothing good ever
comes by certified mail. I have asked several court
clerks for an estimate as to the percentage of certified mail services that are accepted. The consen-
sus is 50%. If you try using the mail to serve your
papers and fail, simply get a process server.
Chances are the defendant will end up paying for it.

NOTE: Never assume that your certified mail
service has been accomplished and show up in court on
the day of the court hearing. If the defendant
didn't sign for the paper, you will be wasting your
time. Call the clerk a couple of days in advance and
find out if the service of process has been completed. This means it must be signed for by the
defendant, not by someone else at the address.

Method 3 Substituted Service (Or "Nail And Mail"):

Often it is hard to serve particular individuals. Some people have developed avoiding the process server into a high (but silly) art. In
California and some other states, this no longer
works as there is now a procedure which allows "substituted service."[2] It works like this in
California:

If a person can't be served with "reasonable
diligence," which is normally interpreted to be three
unsuccessful tries at personal service, the papers

---

2 See California Code of Civil Procedure Section 415.20.

may be served by leaving a copy of the summons and complaint at the person's dwelling place in the presence of a competent member of the household who is at least eighteen years of age and who must be told what the papers are about and thereafter mailing a copy of the summons and complaint by first class mail to the person served. Service is complete ten days after mailing. Be sure that all steps are carried out by a disinterested adult. Because some Small Claims Court clerks interpret the requirement for "due diligence" differently, you will wish to run through the procedure with your local clerk before trying it. If your suit is against a corporation, the substituted service procedure is easier. There is no requirement that you try personal service three times before using substituted service. Papers may be served by leaving a copy of the summons and complaint at the defendant's office with a person apparently in charge of the office during normal business hours and then mailing another copy of the summons and complaint to the person to be served at the same address by first class mail. Service is accomplished ten days after mailing.

After service is accomplished, you must return an affidavit to the court clerk that all proper steps have been accomplished. See Section F, below.

Method 4   For Serving Subpoenas Only:

In Chapter 14 we discuss subpoenaing witnesses and documents. Subpoenas can't be served by mail. They must be served by personal service. The rules as to who can do the serving, etc., are the same as those set forth above in Method 1 with one important difference: any person, including the person bringing the suit, can serve the subpoena. The person making the service must be ready to pay the person subpoenaed a witness fee if it is requested.

C. Costs Of Personal Service

Professional process servers commonly charge
from $14-$25 per service depending on time and mileage
involved.[3] You can usually get your costs of service
added to your judgment if you win, but be sure to
remind the judge to do this when you conclude your
court presentation. However, a few courts, such as
the Berkeley Small Claims Court, will not give the
successful party an award of costs for a process
server unless they have first tried to have the
papers served by the cheaper certified mail approach
(Method 2 above). Other judicial districts such as
Los Angeles prefer that you don't use the mail
approach at all because they feel that too often the
mail isn't accepted. Ask the Small Claims clerk in
your district how they prefer that you accomplish
service and how much the judge will allow as a service of process fee.

---

3 County officials such as sheriffs and marshals will only serve
papers in the county in which they are located. Call them to ask
about fees.

D. Time Limits In Which Papers Must Be Served

The defendant is entitled to receive service of the "Claim of Plaintiff" form at least five days before the date of the court hearing, if he or she is served within the county in which the courthouse is located. If the defendant is served in a county other than the one where the trial is to take place, he must be served at least 15 days before the trial date.

If the defendant is served less than the required number of days before the trial date, he can either go ahead with the trial anyway, or request that the case be delayed (continued) for 10 to 30 days. If it is impossible to show up in person to ask for a delay, call the court clerk (telegraph if you can't call) and point out that you weren't served in the proper time and that you want the case put over. The clerk will see that a default judgment is not entered against you. See Chapter 10 E. But just to be sure get the clerk's name.

To count the days to see if service has been accomplished in the correct time, do not count the day the service is accomplished, but do count the day of the court appearance. Also count weekends and holidays.[4] Thus, if Jack served Julie on July 12 in Los Angeles County, with a "Declaration and Order" listing a July 17 court date in the same county, service would be proper. This is true even if Saturday and Sunday fell on July 14 and 15. To count the days you would not count July 12, the day of service, but you would count July 13, 14, 15, 16, and 17 for a total of five days. If you are unable to serve the defendant(s) within the proper time, simply ask the court clerk for a new court date and try again.

DEFENDANT'S NOTE: If you are improperly served either because you are not given adequate time, or

---

◆ ▽ ◆

---

4 C.C.P. Section 12.

the papers weren't handed to your personally, or a certified letter wasn't signed for by you, it is still wise for you to call the court clerk or show up in court on the day in question. Why should you have to do this if service was improper? Because the plaintiff may succeed in getting the case heard as a default if you fail to show up. It's more trouble to get a default set aside than to protect yourself from the start. But isn't this a Catch-22? You are entitled to proper service, but if you don't get it, you have to show up in court anyway? Perhaps, but as Catch-22's go, this one is mild. You can call the clerk or show up in court and request that the judge grant you a continuance to prepare your case. If the original service was in fact improper, your request will be honored. Of course, if you were improperly served and simply want to get the hearing out of the way, you can show up and go ahead with your case.

E. Serving A Business

If you are suing someone who owns his own business, or is a partner in the business, you must serve the person individually using the rules set out above. However, if you are suing a corporation, the rules are a little different.

Although a corporation is a legal person for purposes of lawsuits, you will still need to have your papers served on someone who lives and breathes. This is true whether you have the papers served personally, or use certified mail.[5] The flesh and blood person should be an officer of the corporation (president, vice-president, secretary or treasurer). Simply call the corporation and ask who, and where, they are. If they won't tell you, the city or county business tax and license people should be able to, at least for local corporations (see Chapter 8). If they can't, the California Secretary of State will supply a "Last Statement of Officers" for a small fee. If you have trouble getting someone at a large

---

5 In Los Angeles and some other California judicial districts, the clerks insist that you use personal service to serve a corporation.

national corporation to accept service, call or write
the California Secretary of State, Corporate Status
Unit, 1230 J Street, Sacramento, California 95814.
They will be able to tell you who is authorized to
accept service for the company in California. You can
do this by phone: (916) 445-2900.[6] If you are suing
a corporation in a situation where you know that the
officers (or general manager) of the corporation work
out of a local office, it is easy to use substituted
service as set out in Method 3 above.

F. Notifying the Court That Service Has Been Accomplished ("Proof Of Service")

Where certified mail is involved, you need do
nothing. The court clerk sends out the certified
mail for you and the signed post office receipt comes
back directly to the clerk if service is accomplished. It's as simple as that.

However, a court has no way of knowing whether
or not papers have been successfully served by personal service unless you tell them. This is done by
filing a piece of paper known as a "Proof of Service"
with the court clerk after the service has been made.
The "Proof of Service" is a small, perforated,
tear-off form that is part of the "Declaration and
Order" package which must be signed by the person
actually making the service. A "Proof of Service" is
used both by the plaintiff and by the defendant if he
files a "counterclaim." It must be returned to the
clerk's office not less than 48 hours before the
trial. A "Proof of Service" is used when any legal
documents are served by personal service. We will
refer back to this example several times in future

---

6 If a corporation has no authorized agent and you can find no corporate officer authorized to accept service in California, there is a
procedure under which you can still accomplish valid service by
"substituted service on the Secretary of State." To do this you must
get a court order from the Small Claims Court clerk. Send this paper
to the Secretary of State with a fee. Unfortunately, while this
accomplishes legal service, it is rarely warranted. Why? Because if
you can't find anyone to serve, it's unlikely you can find assets to
collect from.

chapters. Frequently there isn't time after a
defendant is served for her to properly complete
service of a "Claim of Defendant." In this situation, the defendant should simply file her Claim of
Defendant and bring up the service problem in court.
The plaintiff may well waive the time of service
requirement and agree to proceed. If he doesn't, the
judge will continue the case.

G. Serving A "Claim Of Defendant"

As you will remember from our discussion in
Chapter 9, a "Claim of Defendant" is the form that the
defendant files when he wishes to sue the plaintiff
for money damages arising out of the same incident
that forms the basis for the plaintiff's suit. A
"Claim of Defendant" should be filed with the clerk
and served on the plaintiff at least five days prior
to the time that the court has set for the hearing on
the plaintiff's claim.[7] There will not be time to
serve the "Claim of Defendant" by mail, so you will
have to use personal service, returning a "Proof of
Service" form to the court clerk. If you are a
defendant who has filed a claim and you are unable to
serve the plaintiff, simply show up at the court
hearing date with your papers and serve the plaintiff
in the hallway (not the courtroom). Then explain to
the judge why it was impossible to locate the
plaintiff earlier. The judge will either put the
whole case over a few days, or allow you to proceed
with your claim that day. Either way, he/she will
accept your "Claim of Defendant" as validly served.

H. Serving Someone In The Military— Declaration Of Non-Military Service

It is proper to serve someone who is on active
duty in the armed forces. If he/she shows up, fine.

---

7 If the plaintiff has served the defendant less than 10 days before
the date of the court hearing, the claim of defendant need only be
served on the plaintiff one day prior to the hearing. C.C.P. 116.8.

If he/she doesn't, you have a problem. We learned in Chapter 10 that as a general rule, if a properly served defendant doesn't show up, you can get a "default judgment" against him or her. This is not true if the person you are suing is in the military (the reserves don't count).

Default judgments cannot normally be taken against people in the armed forces because Congress has given our military personnel special protections. To get a default judgment against any defendant a statement must be filed under penalty of perjury that he or she is not in the military. The "Declaration of Non-Military Service" is part of your "Claim of Plaintiff" package and is routinely filled out and signed as part of every case, unless, of course, the defendant is in the military. Clerks accept "Declaration of Non-Military Service" signed by the plaintiff, as long as the plaintiff reasonably believes that the defendant is not on active duty. This constitutes a lenient interpretation of the law by clerks, but no one seems to be complaining

---

IN THE MUNICIPAL COURT, _____ JUDICIAL DISTRICT

OF _____ , STATE OF CALIFORNIA

DECLARATION OF NON-MILITARY SERVICE

No. _____

_____
Plaintiff

vs.

_____
Defendant

County of _____
STATE OF CALIFORNIA, } ss.

The undersigned declares:

1. That ...he is over the age of eighteen years and competent to be a witness in the above entitled action;

2. That this affidavit is made to comply with the provisions of the Act of Congress cited as the Soldiers' and Sailors' Civil Relief Act of 1940, and amendments thereto;

3. That _____ , in the above entitled action, is not in the military service of the United States, within the meaning of said Act, as amended; that said person is not a member of the United States Mar-   Corps Women's Reserve, or Women's Army Auxiliary Corps or Women's Army Corps (W.A.C.S.), or   Coast Guard Reserve (S.P.A.R.S.), or Women's Vol- unteer Naval Reserve (W.A.V.E.S.), or trainin   ·ducated under the supervision of the United States preliminary to induction into the Military Service,   ·nder orders to report for induction under the Selec- tive Training and Service Act of 1940, as amended, or as a member of the En'isted Reserve Corps under orders to report for military service, or an American citizen serving with the forces of any nation allied with the United States in the prosecution of the war, within the purview of the Soldiers' and Sailors' Civil Relief Act of 1940, as amended, or in the Federal Service on active duty as a member of the Army of the United States, or the United States Navy, or the Marine Corps, or the Coast Guard, or as an officer of the Public Health Service.

I declare under penalty of perjury that the foregoing is true and correct.

Executed on _____ at _____ , Calif.
(Date)   (Place)

_____
(Declarant)

203-32 (69)   DECLARATION OF NON-MILITARY SERVICE

12.

The Defendant's Options

This chapter is devoted to a review of the concerns of the defendant. Most of this material has already been discussed in the first eleven chapters, but it will be helpful to pull it all together in one place. Let's start by assuming that you are the person being sued. How do you approach what's happening to you? First, when you receive the plaintiff's papers, you will have to make one of several decisions. There is no one correct course of action--it all depends on your circumstances.

A. Improper Service

You may conclude that the service was not proper (see Chapter 11). Perhaps the "Claim of Plaintiff" was left with your neighbors, or maybe you didn't have the correct number of days in which to respond. You may be tempted not to show up in court, figuring that since you weren't served properly, the case can't be heard. As noted, this is not a smart idea. The judge can easily be unaware of, or overlook, the service problem and issue a default judgment against you. If this happens, you will have to go to the trouble of requesting that the default be set aside. You are better off to contact the clerk, explain the problem with the service and ask that the case be continued to a date that is convenient to you. If the clerk can't help, write the judge or show up on the day in question and request a continuance.

B. No Defense

Now let's assume that the service was OK, but you have no real defense, or don't have the time to defend yourself, or for some other reason don't feel like going to court.[1] A decision not to show up will very likely result in a default judgment being entered against you. It will most probably be for the dollar amount demanded by the plaintiff, plus his or her filing fee and costs to serve you. We discuss default judgments in more detail in Chapters 10 and 15. Basically, a default judgment has the same effect as if you showed up, argued your case and lost.

If you do not dispute the plaintiff's claim, but cannot afford to pay it all at once, your best bet is to show up in court and explain your situation to the judge. If you can't be present, ask the clerk if there is a form for you to fill out to do this in writing. If there isn't, write a letter to the court prior to the court hearing (be sure to properly identify the case, using the number from the Claim of Plaintiff form.) When the judge enters a judgment against you, he or she has the power to order that you pay in monthly installments and probably will do so.

---

1 Many people are tempted not to show up and defend a case in Small Claims Court because they have no money and figure that even if they lose, the plaintiff can't collect. This is "grasshopper thinking." The sun may be shining today and the judgment may cause you no immediate problem. But remember, judgments are good for ten years and can be renewed for another ten. You may put a few nickels together sometime in the future and you probably won't want them taken away by an industrious little ant holding a Small Claims judgment in his mouth. So wake up and defend yourself while you can.

C. Try To Compromise

If you feel that perhaps the plaintiff has some right on his or her side, but that you are being sued for too much, contact the plaintiff and try to work out a compromise settlement. Any settlement you make should be set down in writing along the lines outlined in Chapter 6. It should also include a specific statement that the plaintiff will forever drop his pending lawsuit. Simply add a clause like the following to the sample agreement outlined in Chapter 6.

> "As part of this settlement (name of plaintiff) hereby agrees to drop the lawsuit, number (insert number) filed in Small Claims Court in the _____ judicial district on ___(date)___ against (name of defendant) and that no further court action(s) will be filed regarding the subject matter of this agreement."

As a practical matter any lawsuit that is not actively prosecuted will be dropped by the clerk. The reason that you want to have a settlement agreement written out is to cover the unlikely possibility that the other party will accept money from you and then try to go ahead with his suit too. If this happens, you need only show your written settlement agreement to the judge.

D. Fight Back

Now we get to those of you who feel that you don't owe the plaintiff a dime. You will want to actively fight. This means that you must show up in court on the date stated in the papers served on you unless you get the case continued (see Chapter 10). A defendant need not file any papers with the court clerk; showing up ready to defend yourself is enough. The strategies to properly argue a case, including the presentation of witnesses, estimates, diagrams, etc. arc discussed in Chapters 13-22 and apply

equally to defendants and plaintiffs. You will wish
to study this information carefully and develop a
strategy for your case. You will also want to see
whether the plaintiff has brought the case within the
time allowed by the Statute of Limitations (Chapter
5) and whether he has asked for a reasonable amount
of money (Chapter 4). If you simply show up without
thinking out a coherent presentation, you are likely
to lose.

E. File A "Claim Of Defendant"

Finally, there are those of you who not only
want to dispute the plaintiff's claim, but also want
to sue him. This involves promptly filing a "Claim
of Defendant" for up to $1,500 in Small Claims Court,
or for a larger amount in Municipal or Superior
Court. See Chapters 10 C and 11 G for more details.

13.

Getting Ready for Court

Once you have your papers on file and the
defendant(s) served, the preliminaries are over and
you are ready for the main event--your day in court.
Movies, and especially T.V., have done much to make
court proceedings false. Ask yourself, what was a
trial like before every lawyer fancied himself
Raymond Burr or Charles Laughton and judges acted
"fatherly," or "stern," or "indignantly outraged"?

There are people whose lives revolve around
courthouses, and who have been playing movie parts
for so long that they have become caricatures of one
screen star or another. Lawyers are particularly
susceptible to this virus. All too often they substitute posturing and theatrics for good hard preparation. Thankfully though, most people who work in
our courts quickly recover from movieitis and realize
that the majestic courtroom is in truth a large,
drafty hall with a raised platform at one end: His

honor is only a lawyer dressed in a black shroud who knew the right politician and that they themselves are not bit players in "Witness For The Prosecution," "Inherit the Wind" or "The Verdict."

I mention movieitis because it's a common ailment in Small Claims Court. Cases that should be easily won are often lost because somebody goes marching around the courtroom antagonizing everyone with comic opera imitations of E. G. Marshall. And don't assume that you are immune. Movieitis is a subtle disease because people often don't realize they have it. Ask yourself a few self-diagnostic questions. Have you watched courtroom scenes on T.V. or in the movies? Have you ever imagined that you were one of the actor-lawyers? How many times have you been in a real courtroom in comparison to watching movie set courtrooms?

My purpose here is not to lecture you on how to present yourself in court. But perhaps I can get you to remember something that you already know--you don't need to be false to yourself to succeed in Small Claims Court. You don't need to put on fancy clothes or airs, or try to appear more polished, intelligent or sophisticated than you are. Be yourself and you will do just fine. If you have a chance, go to the court a few days before your case is heard and watch for an hour or two. You may not learn a great deal that will be helpful in your case, but you will be a lot more relaxed and comfortable when your turn comes. Watching a few cases is a particularly good thing to do if you feel anxious about your court appearance. For those of you who love to act, who simply can't pass up an opportunity to perform, at least act real. That's right, go ahead and act if you must; but make your performance that of a person--not a personality.

Movieitis aside, most people I have watched in Small Claims Court have done extremely well. Many mornings I have been inspired, feeling that for the first time in years I have seen honesty and truth put in an appearance before the Bar of Justice. This truly surprised me as I had hardly ever taken the time to watch a Small Claims case before doing research for this book. I stopped taking clients several years ago, in part, because I hated the dishonest sham that goes on in the courtroom--hated the endless natterings between lawyers about logic-chopping technicalities while clients paid and paid and paid. It was wonderful to see that once the lawyers were removed and people began communicating directly, there was much about our court system that made sense.

Commonly a judge must decide a case, at least in part, on the basis of who seems to be the most believable. This is because there isn't enough hard evidence to be conclusive either way. Different judges have varying prejudices, hunches, feelings, etc., about who is, or isn't telling the truth. Often they themselves can't explain the many intangibles that go into making this sort of decision, but most agree that the more honestly a person presents himself/herself, the more likely he or she is to be believed. For example, a house painter who shows up in his overalls and puts his lunchbox under the chair will probably be much more convincing (and comfortable) than he would be if he came painfully squeezed into his blue wedding and funeral suit. As one judge told me, "A pimp being a pimp has as good a chance as anyone else in my courtroom, but a pimp who tries to act like Saint Paul better watch out."

Before we get into a discussion of how to prepare and present different types of cases, here are a few general suggestions:

A. Interpreter Services

The Small Claims Court clerk is required to maintain and make available a list of interpreters in as many languages as possible who are willing to aid parties for no fee or a reasonable fee. However, failure to have an interpreter for a particular language on the list shall not invalidate any proceedings. (C.C.P. 117.16.)

B. Court Times

Small Claims courts can schedule cases any time they wish on business days. Most commonly court is held at 9:00 A.M. In larger judicial districts, Saturday or evening sessions must also be held.

C. Free Small Claims Advice

Every county must provide a program of free advice to Small Claims litigants on how to present their claims or defenses in Small Claims Court. Code of Civil Procedure Section 117.18 requires an "advisory service" be provided "in person, by telephone, or by any other means reasonably calculated to provide timely and appropriate assistance." Some counties such as Marin and San Francisco take this mandate seriously and provide a thorough service with convenient hours. Others such as Alameda and Napa provide little help. Ask the clerk about times and places for your local advisory programs. Those giving advice may be law students, paralegals, or--you guessed it--lawyers. I am extremely worried and cynical about the introduction of lawyers into the Small Claims process.[1] One of the main advantages of Small Claims has been to get away from lawyers, and every time I think of them starting to get involved in Small Claims, I think of what eventually happened when the Arab let the camel put his nose in the tent. If you are in Los Angeles, San Jose or San Diego and want more information about their conciliation programs, contact the Small Claims Court clerk.

---

[1] The California Bar Association has supported legislation adding lawyers to the Small Claims process and many lawyers in the legislature have been involved in its passage. I believe that it is a serious conflict of interest for lawyer-legislators to vote on Small Claims bills, especially when the effect is to make more jobs for lawyers. As I discuss in Chapter 25, I believe that arbitration and mediation approaches would be helpful in Small Claims Court, but why not have them provided by non-lawyers?

D. Getting To The Courthouse

Before you get to the right courtroom, you have
to get to the right building. Small Claims courts
are often not in the main courthouse, but like a half
forgotten stepsister, are housed wherever there's an
empty room. Don't assume that you know where to go
if you haven't been there before. Plaintiffs have
already had to find the clerk's office, so they
probably know where the courtroom is, but defendants
should check this out. Be sure too, that your witnesses know exactly where and when to show up. And do
plan to be on time--people who rush in flustered and
late start with a strike against them.

NOTE: San Francisco and some other counties use
an insulting hurry-up-and-wait technique that would
make the Army blush. They have everyone show up at
8:15 A.M. in one large room. At this time the judges
are still home having coffee. Court is supposed to
start at 9:00, although 9:15 is normal, and 9:30 is
all too common. Can you imagine the court making
lawyers show up an hour early for no reason? Courts
sometimes begin at 8:30, but far more often at 9:00
in the morning--if they tell you an earlier time,
call them up and ask what time the judge really gets
there.

E. Understanding The Courtroom

Most Small Claims proceedings are conducted in
standard courthouses that are also used for other
purposes. Indeed, sometimes you will have to sit
through a few minutes of some other type of court
proceedings before the Small Claims calendar is
called.

Most judges still sit on high in their little,
wooden throne boxes, and most still wear those
depressing black judicial robes that trace their
history back over a thousand years to an England in
which courts were largely controlled by king, nobility and clergy. There are no laws requiring these

THE JUDGE:
IDENTIFIES THE PEOPLE INVOLVED. HEARS TESTIMONY. LOOKS AT DOCUMENTS AND DECIDES THE CASE.

THE ROBE:
HIGH FASHION IN THE MIDDLE AGES. PERHAPS A BIT SILLY TODAY, BUT SEEMS TO MAKE THE JUDGE FEEL IMPORTANT.

THE CLERK:
ANNOUNCES THE CASE. COLLECTS AND MARKS THE DOCUMENTARY EVIDENCE.

THE BAILIFF
GENERALLY DOES NOTHING, BUT IS PRESENT TO PRESERVE ORDER.

out-of-date traditions, and a few judges prefer to conduct their court more informally. In addition to the judge, a clerk and a bailiff will normally be present. They sit at tables immediately in front of the judge. The clerk's job is to keep the judge supplied with necessary files and papers, and to make sure that proceedings flow smoothly. A clerk is not the same as a court reporter who keeps a word-by-word record of proceedings. No such record is kept in Small Claims Court, and no court reporter is present.

Courtrooms are divided about two-thirds of the way toward the front by a little fence. This fence is known to initiates as the "bar." The public must stay on the opposite side of the bar from the judge, clerk, bailiff, attorneys, etc., unless invited to cross. This invitation occurs when your case is called by the clerk. At this point you come forward and sit at the long table (known as the counsel table) just inside the fence.[2] You and your witnesses sit facing the judge with your backs to the

---

2 In a few courtrooms judges try to hurry things by asking everyone to stand in front of the Judges Bench. The idea seems to be if people can't sit down they will present their cases faster. This might be O.K. if the judge would stand too. As it is, I feel it's insulting.

rest of the courtroom. In most Small Claims Courts, you will have been sworn (or affirmed if you wish) to tell the truth before the judge arrives. If this has not already been done, the oath will be administered at this time. In the great majority of Small Claims Courts you, your opponent and your witnesses will present the entire case from the long table. This means that you do not sit in the witness box next to the judge. Many people feel that it is polite to stand when addressing the judge, but you should do what feels most comfortable to you.

When your case is called and you come forward to take your turn at the counsel table, have all your papers with you ready to present to the judge. This can include bills, receipts, estimates, photographs, contracts, letters to or from your opponent, etc.

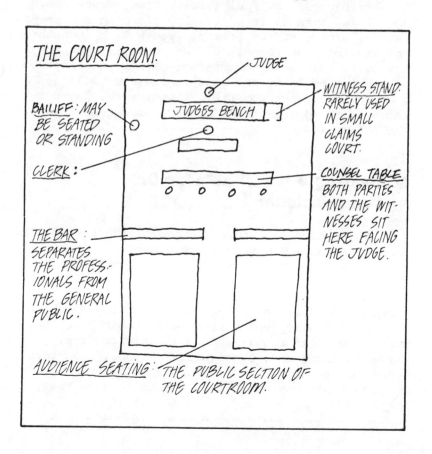

THE COURT ROOM.

JUDGE

WITNESS STAND: RARELY USED IN SMALL CLAIMS COURT.

BAILIFF: MAY BE SEATED OR STANDING

JUDGES BENCH

CLERK:

COUNSEL TABLE BOTH PARTIES AND THE WITNESSES SIT HERE FACING THE JUDGE.

THE BAR: SEPARATES THE PROFESSIONALS FROM THE GENERAL PUBLIC.

AUDIENCE SEATING: THE PUBLIC SECTION OF THE COURTROOM.

When the time comes to show these to the judge, you
simply hand them to the clerk who will pass them on
to the judge. As I have said before, documentation
is a great aid to your case, but don't go overboard.
Judges are a little like donkeys--load them too
heavily and they are likely to lie down and go to
sleep.

F. Dealing With Your Opponent

Before you get to the courtroom, you should do a
little thinking about your opponent. Perhaps you can
guess what sort of presentation he or she will make.
If so, ask yourself how you can best deal with these
arguments. This may be a good way to take the negative energy you may feel (frustration, annoyance,
anger) and turn it into creative planning and preparation. In court, be polite. You will gain nothing,
and may lose the respect of the judge, if you are
obviously hostile or sarcastic. Don't interrupt your
opponent when he or she is speaking--you will get
your chance. When you present your case, lay out the
facts to the judge; don't conduct an argument with
the other side.

G. Dealing With The Judge Or Commissioner[3]

It is hard to generalize about judges--each is
an individual. I have seen more good than bad, but
that doesn't help if your case comes up before an
idiot. Unlike higher courts, no great intellectual
ability is required to be a good Small Claims Court
judge--indeed, most of the judges sitting on the
United States Supreme Court would probably be lousy
at it. What is required is a liking for people,
openmindedness and, above all, patience. Everyone
who comes to Small Claims Court should have the
feeling that they got a fair chance to have their
say.

---

3 Commissioners are appointed court personnel empowered to hear
Small Claims Court cases.

Most Small Claims Court judges are judges in the more formal Municipal Courts who also hear the Small Claims calendar. This is a mistake. The last thing that is needed in Small Claims Court is the "me judge, you peasant" philosophy of our formal court system. Hopefully as Small Claims Court expands in the future, it will be staffed by people (not necessarily lawyers) specifically trained to meet its needs (see Chapter 25).

Lawyers are often appointed as temporary judges in Small Claims.[4] The legal slang for a temporary judge is "Judge, pro tem." If your case comes up on a day when there is a "Judge, pro tem," you have one small advantage: you can choose whether or not to have your case heard by that particular person. How does this work? Under the law you can ask that the hearing be delayed until a regular judge is available. Simply sit and watch the cases that are heard before yours. If the judge seems O.K. to you, go ahead when your turn comes. But, if for some reason you don't like the "pro tem" judge, ask that your case be delayed until another day.

What if it's a regular judge—or commissioner— you don't like after having seen a few cases before yours? A little-known law (C.C.P. 170.6) allows you to "disqualify" a judge simply on your honest belief that s/he is "prejudiced" against you. To do this, you can simply say, when your case is called (after you've been "sworn in"), something like, "Your Honor, I believe you are prejudiced against my interest, and I request a trial before another judge."

When thinking about presenting your case to a judge, there is one constructive thing that you can do. Imagine yourself in the judge's shoes. What would you value most from the people appearing before you? Before I ever sat as a judge, my answer was politeness, good organization of the material to be presented and reasonable brevity. After experiencing Small Claims Court from the judge's chair, I would

● ● ● ● ● ▽▼▽ ● ● ● ● ●

---

4 Court commissions also hear Small Claims cases. Commissions can be challenged following the same rules that apply to judges.

only add--documented evidence. By this, I mean evidence that is supported by more than the word of the person bringing, or defending, the case. Witnesses, written statements, police accident reports, photographs--all these give the judge a chance to make a decision on something more than who tells the best story. And one final thing. Remember, the judge has heard thousands of stories very much like yours and will either cease paying attention or get annoyed if you try repeating your story three times.

14.

Witnesses

It is often helpful to have someone in court
with you who has a first hand knowledge of the facts
of your case and who can support your point of view.
In many types of cases, such as car accidents, or
disputes concerning whether or not a tenant left an
apartment clean, witnesses are particularly valuable.
In other fact situations, they aren't as necessary.
For example, if a friend borrowed $500 and didn't pay
it back, you don't need a witness to prove that your
friend's (ex-friend's?) signature on the promissory
note is genuine unless you expect him to base his
defense on the theory that his signature was forged.

To arrange for a witness, simply talk to people
you believe have something helpful to say and see if
they will come down to the court and say it. You
should do this even though subpoena forms are available from the Small Claims clerk's office to require
a person's presence (see A below for details). Subpoenas are helpful when a person would otherwise have

difficulty getting off school or work, but should
almost never be used to drag someone in who doesn't
want to come. Courts have lists of interpreters
available if there is a language difficulty, but you
should contact them well in advance if an interpreter
will be needed.

    A good witness should have first hand knowledge
of the facts in dispute. This means that he or she
saw the car accident, or the dog bite, or the dirty
apartment, etc. The judge will not be interested in
the testimony of a person who is repeating second
hand or generalized information such as, "I know Joe
is a good, safe driver and would never have done
anything reckless," or "I didn't see Joe's apartment
before he moved out, but both Joe and his mother, who
couldn't be here today, told me that they worked for
two days cleaning it up."

subpoenaed witness is entitled to a small witness fee
(see A below);

   * Never use a subpoena form to require a witness to be present unless you have made sure that it
is O.K. with the witness (more in A below).

   Prepare your witness thoroughly as to what your
position is, what your opponent is likely to say and
what you want the witness to say. In court, the
witness will be on his/her own and you want to be
sure that the story comes out right. It is completely legal to thoroughly discuss the case with the
witness beforehand.

   IMPORTANT: In court a witness will be pretty
much on his or her own. The witness will sit with
you at the table facing the judge. Normally a witness doesn't take the witness stand in Small Claims.
Most judges prefer that you don't pretend to be a
lawyer and ask the witness a lot of questions. Simply let the witness explain what happened as he or
she saw it. The judge may ask the witness questions.
If you feel that the witness has left something out,
you should ask a question designed to produce the
information that you want.

A. Subpoenaing Witnesses

   In California and most other states, you can
require that a witness be present if that person
resides within the state. To do this, go to the
clerk's office and get a "Subpoena" form. Fill it
out, and have it served on the person who you wish to
have present. But remember, you never want to subpoena a person unless you have talked to him/her
first and gotten an O.K. The very act of dragging
someone into court who doesn't want to come may set
him/her against you. A subpoenaed witness is
entitled to a fee of $35.00 and $.40 per mile. If
you win your case, you will probably be able to
recover your witness fees from the other side. The

A good witness is believable. This isn't always
a quality of easy definition--a policeman may be a
symbol of honesty to some people, while others regard
him or her with hostility and fear. But remember, it
is the judge you are trying to convince and judges
tend to be fairly establishment folk (they make comfortable salaries, own their own homes and generally
tend to like the existing order of things). Most
judges I know would tend to believe a policeman.

In many types of cases such as a car accident,
you won't have much choice as to witnesses. You will
be lucky to have one. But in other disputes (was the
house properly painted, or the work on the car engine
completed?), you have an opportunity to plan ahead.
When you do, try to get a witness who is particularly
knowledgeable about the dispute in question. Thus,
in a dispute over whether car repairs were properly
done, bring a working car mechanic rather than your
neighbor "who knows a lot about cars." Close friends
and family are often your only witnesses. There is
no rule that says that you can't have these people
testify for you. Indeed, I have often seen a person's spouse, or the friend that he/she lives with,
give very convincing testimony. But, given a choice,
it is better to have a witness who is not your close
friend or kin. A judge may discount testimony of
people to whom you are close on the theory that they
would naturally be biased in your favor.

I will talk more about witnesses as I go through
the various case examples (Chapters 16-21), but let's
outline a few basic do's and don'ts here:

* Never bring a witness to court who is hostile
to you or hostile to the idea of testifying;

* Never bring a witness to court unless you
know exactly what he or she will say. This sounds
basic, but I have seen people lose cases because
their witnesses supported the other side or got mixed
up;

* It's not illegal to pay an expert witness
(say a car mechanic who has examined your engine). A

PLAINTIFF:
Public Library

DEFENDANT:
John O'Gara

CIVIL SUBPENA ☑COURT ☐DEPOSITION	CASE NUMBER:
☐DUCES TECUM ☐OTHER (specify):	(Fill in number)

THE PEOPLE OF THE STATE OF CALIFORNIA, TO (NAME):

(Name of witness you wish to subpena)

1. **YOU ARE ORDERED TO APPEAR AS A WITNESS in this action as follows unless you make a special agreement with the person named in item 3:**

   a. Date: Time: ☐ Dept.:   ☐ Div.:   ☐ Room:

   b. Address:

2. **and you are**

   a. ☑ ordered to appear in person.

   b. ☐ not required to appear in person if you produce the records described in the accompanying affidavit in compliance with Evidence Code sections 1560 and 1561.

   c. ☐ ordered to appear in person and to produce the records described in the accompanying affidavit. The personal attendance of the custodian or other qualified witness and the production of the original records is required by this subpena. The procedure authorized pursuant to subdivision (b) of section 1560, and sections 1561 and 1562, of the Evidence Code will not be deemed sufficient compliance with this subpena.

   d. ☐ ordered to designate one or more persons to testify on your behalf as to the matters described in the accompanying statement. (Code of Civil Procedure 2019(a)(6))

3. **IF YOU HAVE ANY QUESTIONS ABOUT WITNESS FEES OR THE TIME OR DATE FOR YOU TO APPEAR, OR IF YOU WANT TO BE CERTAIN THAT YOUR PRESENCE IS REQUIRED, CONTACT THE ATTORNEY REQUESTING THIS SUBPENA, NAMED ABOVE, OR THE FOLLOWING PERSON, BEFORE THE DATE ON WHICH YOU ARE TO APPEAR:**

   a. Name: John O'Gara   b. Telephone number: 548-1921

4. **WITNESS FEES:** You are entitled to receive witness fees and mileage actually traveled, one way, as provided by law, if you request them **BEFORE** your scheduled appearance. **Request them from the person named in item 3.**

5. If this subpena requires your attendance at proceedings out of court and you refuse to answer questions or sign as required by law, you must attend a court hearing at a time to be fixed by the person conducting such proceedings.

6. You are ordered to appear in this civil matter in your capacity as a peace officer or other person described in Government Code section 68097.1.

   Date: Clerk of the Court, by _____ , Deputy

DISOBEDIENCE OF THIS SUBPENA MAY BE PUNISHED AS CONTEMPT BY THIS COURT. YOU WILL ALSO BE LIABLE FOR THE SUM OF FIVE HUNDRED DOLLARS AND ALL DAMAGES RESULTING FROM YOUR FAILURE TO OBEY.

For Court Use Only   Dated: . . . . _____
                                    (Signature of person issuing subpena)

                                  . . . . _____
                                    (Type or print name)

                                    . . . . _____
                                    (Title)

(See reverse for proof of service)

Form Adopted by Rule 982
Judicial Council of California
Revised Effective July 1, 1980   **CIVIL SUBPENA**

judge has discretion as to whether to grant you your
witness fees. Some judges are strict about this,
making the loser pay the winner's witness fees only
if he or she finds that the subpoenaed witness was
essential to the presentation of the case. This means
that, if your case is so strong that you don't need a
witness but you subpoena one anyway, you may well
have to pay the witness fee even though you win the
case.

Here is the standard California subpoena form.
You will need to prepare an original and two copies.
Once prepared, take the subpoena form to the Small
Claims Court clerk who will issue it. Service must
be made personally and the "Proof of Service," which
is on the back of the subpoena, returned to the
clerk's office. Rules for service are discussed in
Chapter 11.

B. Subpoenaing Police Officers

You have probably already noticed that on the
subpoena form there is a special box to use if you
wish to subpoena a police officer. The box is easy
to fill out, but hard to pay for. The deposit to
subpoena a police officer is at least $125. This
money must be paid to the clerk at the time the subpoena is issued. Depending on the amount of the
officer's time that is used, you may eventually get a
refund of some of your deposit.

C. Subpoenaing Documents

In addition to witnesses, you can also subpoena
documents. It is rare that this is done in Small
Claims Court, but it may occasionally be helpful.
Someone (police department, phone company, hospital,
corporation) may have certain books, ledgers, papers
or other documents that can help your case. To get
them, you must prepare a form entitled "Subpoena
Duces Tecum." This is very similar to the standard
subpoena form, except that there is a space to
describe the papers or other documents that you want
brought to court. To get a "Subpoena Duces Tecum"
issued, you must attach a declaration stating why you
need the written material. Prepare three copies of
all papers and, after you get the clerk to issue the
subpoena, serve it on the witness using personal
service as described in Chapter 11. To comply with
the subpoena, the custodian of the records may mail
them to court unless you demand the custodian show up

personally.   See C.C.P. 1985; Evidence Code 1560-
1566.[1]

A Subpoena Duces Tecum must be directed to the
person who is in charge of the documents, books or
records that you want.   It may take a few phone calls
to find out who this is.   Be sure you get this
information accurately.   If you list someone on the
"Subpoena Duces Tecum" who has nothing to do with the
documents, you won't get them.   When dealing with a
large corporation, public utility, municipal government, etc., it is wise to list the person who is in
overall charge of the department where the records
are kept.   Thus, if you want records from a public
library having to do with library fines, or from the
city tax and license department having to do with
business license fees, you should not list the city
manager or the mayor, but should list the head
librarian or the director of the tax and license
office.

EXAMPLE: Let's take a hypothetical case.   You
are being sued by the city on behalf of the public
library for $300 for eight rare books which they
state you failed to return.   You know that you did
return the books, but can't seem to get that across
to the library which insists on treating you like a
thief.   You learn that each April the library takes a
yearly inventory of all books on their shelves.   You
believe that, if you can get access to that inventory, you may be able to figure out where the library
misplaced the books.   Your first step is to ask the
library to voluntarily open the inventory to you.   If
they refuse, you may well want to subpoena them.
Here's how to do it:

1.   Check the "Duces Tecum" box on the Subpoena
form.   Check either box 2b or 2c.

2.   Prepare a Declaration.   It should be brief.
Describe the documents you need and why they are

---

1 Evidence Code Section 1563 establishes fees for subpoenaing documents.   These include photocopy fees, compensation for the time of
the record gatherer and a witness fee if you require the custodian of
the documents to appear in court personally.

necessary to prove issues involved in the case. If you want the custodian to show up in person give a reason. Don't argue the merits of your case. See sample below.

4. Staple your Declaration to the Subpoena Duces Tecum form and have the subpoena issued by the Small Claims clerk. Then have the subpoena served, being sure that the "Proof of Service" (see Chapter 11 F) is properly filled out and returned to the clerk.

Name and Address of Attorney: Telephone: For court use only:
    John O'Gara
    15 Scenic St., Los Angeles, CA 90011
Attorney for: IN PRO PER

Plaintiff:
        Public Library

Defendant:
        John O'Gara

DECLARATION FOR: Case Number:
        SUBPENA DUCES TECUM [X]   (Fill in number)
        SUBPENA DUCES TECUM RE: DESPOSITION [ ]

I hereby declare, under penalty of perjury, that I am the attorney of record for
appearing in pro per _____ in the above entitled action;
____ That the deposition of ____not applicable_____ is noticed for
hearing before _____
on _____ at _____.m., at _____
_____ in the city of _____, California.
____ That said action is set for trial on (fill in dates etc.)_____ at _____.m.,
at _____ in the city of _____,
California.
That _Robert Riwgle_____ is a material witness in said action,
and has under his control the following books, documents, or other thing(s):
    Book inventory information collected by the main branch of the public
    library during the calendar year 19___.
That said matters or things are material to the issues involved in said action by
reason of the following facts:*   My contention is that I returned the books which the
    library is suing me for. The inventory should back me up on this.

Request is made that Subpena Duces Tecum issue accordingly.
Executed on_____ at _____, California.

_____

*Materiality must be set forth in full detail

NOTE: The person who you have subpoenaed the
documents from should mail them to the court. If you
need an opportunity to examine the documents, request
it from the judge. He or she may well let you do
your examining right there in the courtroom while
other cases go ahead, or, if necessary, he may continue the case for a few days and arrange to have you
make your examination at the place of business of the
owner of the records.

D. Judges As Witnesses

California Code of Civil Procedure Section 117
states, "The judge may consult witnesses informally
and otherwise investigate the controversy." In
practice this means as much, or as little, as an
individual judge wants it to mean. But it clearly
does allow the conscientious judge great discretion
to climb down off the bench to check out an important
fact.

Using a judge as a witness is a valuable technique in many situations. This is done routinely in
many types of disputes, such as clothing cases in
which you bring the damaged garment into court for
the judge's examination. As I have said repeatedly
in this book, always bring into court any physical
evidence that will help your case and fit through the
door.

But what if your evidence won't fit through the
door (a car with a poor paint job) or can't be
brought into the building (a supposedly pedigreed
puppy that grew up looking as if Lassie were the
mother and Rin Tin Tin the father)? Why not ask the
judge to accompany you outside the building to examine the car, or the dog, or whatever else is important to your case? Many (but not all) judges are
willing to do so if they feel that it is necessary to
a better understanding of the case and won't take too
long. But never ask a judge to take time to leave
his or her court to view evidence if you can prove
your case just as well by other means, such as witnesses and pictures. A good approach is to do as

well as you can in court, and to ask the judge to view evidence outside of court only if it is essential.

E. Testimony By Telephone

A Small Claims Court judge has the power to take testimony or otherwise investigate a case over the phone. Many judges don't like to do this, but a number will if a witness cannot be present because he or she is ill, disabled, out-of-state, or can't take off from work. While procedures vary, some courts will set up conference calls so that the opposing party has the opportunity to hear what is being said and to respond.

Don't just assume that a particular judge will allow information to be presented over the phone. Ask the clerk. If you get a negative response, don't give up--ask the judge when you get into the courtroom. It is also an extremely good idea to have a letter from the witness who you want to reach by phone, explaining what he or she will testify to (e.g., your opponent's car ran a red light and broadsided you) and explaining why it is impossible for him or her to be in court. Such a letter might look like this.

---

37 Ogden Court
Ukiah, CA

Presiding Judge
Small Claims Court
Ukiah, California

Your Honor:

September 30, 19--

Re: John Swift vs.
     Peter Patrakos
     Case # 11478

On September 15, 19--, I witnessed an auto accident at the corner of Hennepin and Eighth in Ukiah, involving John Swift and Peter Patrakos. I clearly saw Mr. Patrokos' car, which was heading north on South Dora, go through a red light and hit Mr. Swift's blue van which was proceeding south on West 7th, well inside the 30 MPH speed limit.

Mr. Swift has asked me to testify on his behalf, and normally I would be happy to do so. However, I will be in New York City on business during the months of October, November and December 19-- and cannot be present.

I have asked Mr. Swift to let me know the day and approximate time of the court hearing and have told him that I will give him a phone number where I can be reached. If you think it desireable, I will be pleased to give my testimony by phone.

Sincerely,

Victor Van Cleve

15.

Presenting Your Case to the Judge

A. Uncontested Cases—Getting A Judgment By Default

Surprisingly often, presenting your case will be easy--your opponent will simply not show up. If this occurs, you will not have to make a formal presentation of your entire case. The judge will check to see that your opponent was properly served and may ask you a question or two to make sure that there is no obvious flaw in your case such as the Statute of Limitations having run out two years ago. He or she will also ask you to present the basic facts of your case briefly, but will not want a long argument or lots of evidence.[1] It's as if you were scheduled to play a ballgame and the other team failed to show up. You win by default--you don't need to hit the ball over the fence and run around the bases. And there is no appeal from a default judgment. If a defendant doesn't show up to argue his case, he can't appeal to the appellate division of the Superior Court (see Chapter 22).

---

1 C.C.P. Section 117(a).

Very occasionally a person who has defaulted
will show up in court a few days later with a super
excuse. The judge does have the discretion to set
aside a default in this situation and re-open the
case. This is rarely done and in no case will it be
done if the defaulting party delays in requesting
that the judgment be set aside. For example, if the
defaulting party shows up three weeks after a default
judgment was entered to request that it be set aside,
he would have the burden of explaining to the judge
why he didn't show up or phone earlier. As you might
guess, not many people can lift a burden this heavy.
(We discuss the mechanics of setting aside a default
in Chapter 10 E). In almost all situations, motions
to set aside defaults _must_ be made within 30 days
after the default was entered.

B. Contested Cases

Assuming now that both sides show up and step
forward when the case is called by the clerk, what
happens next? First, the judge will establish
everyone's identity. Next, he will ask the plaintiff
to briefly state his case.

The plaintiff should tell the judge what is in
dispute and then briefly outline his position. It is
critical that the judge know what the case is about
before you start arguing it. For example, if your
case involves a car accident, you might start by
saying, "This case involves a car accident at Cedar
and Rose Streets in which my car suffered $372 worth
of damage," not "It all started when I was driving
down Rose Street after having two eggs and a danish
for breakfast." Only occasionally have I seen a case
where the plaintiff's initial presentation should
take longer than five minutes. As part of his or her
statement the plaintiff should present any papers,
photos or other documentary evidence. These should
be handed to the clerk and explained. The plaintiff
should also be sure to indicate the presence of any
witnesses to the judge.

When the plaintiff is finished, the judge may
wish to ask questions. He or she may or may not wish
to hear from the plaintiff's witnesses before the
defendant speaks. Each judge will control the flow
of evidence differently. It's best to go with the
judge's energy, not against it. Just be sure that,
at one time or another, you have made all of your
points. If you feel rushed, say so. The judge will
normally slow things down a little.

Sooner or later the defendant will get his
chance. Defendants often get so angry at something
the plaintiff has said ("lies! lies!") that when
their turn comes, they immediately attack. This is
silly and usually counter-productive. The defendant
should calmly and clearly present his side of the
dispute to the judge. If the plaintiff has made
false or misleading statements, these should be
answered, but at the end of the presentation, not at
the beginning. Tell your story first, then deal with
the plaintiff's testimony if this seems necessary.

Here are a few tips that you may find helpful.
These are not rules written on golden tablets, but
only suggestions. You may want to follow some and
ignore others.

1. Stand when you make your initial presentation to the judge. Standing gives most people a
sense of presence and confidence at a time when they
may be a little nervous. But this doesn't mean that
you have to jump to your feet every time the judge
asks you a question.

2. Don't read your statement. Reading in court
is almost always a bore. Some people find it helpful
to make a few notes on a card to serve as a reminder
if they get nervous or forget something. If you
decide to do this, list the headings of the various
points you want to make in an outline form. Be sure
your list is easy to read at a glance and that the
topics are in the correct order.

3. Be brief.

4. Never interrupt your opponent or any of the witnesses no matter how outrageous their "lies." You will get your chance to respond.

5. Be prepared to present any section of your case that is difficult to get across in words, in another way. This means bringing your used car parts, damaged clothing or other exhibits, such as photographs or cancelled checks with you, and having them organized for easy presentation.

6. There will be a blackboard in court. If a drawing would be helpful, as they almost always are in cases involving car accidents, be sure that you have practiced at home. You will want to draw clearly and legibly the first time. If you wish to make a drawing and the judge doesn't ask you to, simply request permission to do so.

A Sample Contested Case: Now let's take a typical case and pretend that a court reporter is making a transcript.

Clerk: "The next case is John Andrews v. Robertson Realty. Will everyone please come forward?" (Four people come forward and sit at the table facing the judge.)

Judge: "Good morning. Which one of you is Mr. Andrews? O.K., will you begin, Mr. Andrews?"

John Andrews: (stands) "This is a case about my failure to get a $400 cleaning deposit returned, your Honor. I rented a house from Robertson Realty at 1611 Spruce St. in Fresno in March of 198_, on a month-to-month tenancy. On January 10, 198_, I sent Mr. Robertson a written notice that I was planning to move on March 10. In fact, I moved out on March 8 and left the place extremely clean. All of my rent was properly paid. A few days after I moved out, I asked Mr. Robertson to return my $400 deposit. He refused, saying that the place was dirty and that he was keeping my deposit.

I have with me a copy of a letter I wrote to Mr. Robertson on March 15 setting out my position in more detail. I also have some photographs that my friend Carol Spann, who is here as a witness, took on the day I moved out. I believe the pictures show pretty clearly that I did a thorough clean-up. (John Andrews hands the letter and pictures to the clerk who hands them to the judge.)

Your Honor, I am asking not only for the $400 deposit, but also for $200 in punitive damages that the law allows a tenant when a landlord improperly refuses to return a deposit." [2]

Judge: "Mr. Andrews, will you introduce your witness."

Andrews: "Yes, this is Carol Spann. She helped me clean up and move on March 7 and 8."

Judge: (looking at the pictures) "Ms. Spann, were you in the apartment the day John Andrews moved out?"

Carol Spann: (standing) "Yes, I was and the day before too. I helped clean up and I can say that we did a good job. Not only did we do the normal washing and scrubbing, but we waxed the kitchen floor and shampooed the rugs."

Judge: (turning to Mr. Robertson) "O.K., now it's your turn to tell me why the deposit wasn't returned."

Harry Robertson: (standing) "I don't know how they could have cleaned the place up, your Honor, because it was filthy when I inspected it on March 9. Let me give you a few specifics. There was mildew and mold around the bathtub, the windows were filthy, the refrigerator hadn't been defrosted and there was dog--how shall I say it--dog manure in the basement.

---

[2] The legal rules on returning deposits and punitive damages are contained in Section 1950.5 of the California Civil Code and are particularly described in Chapter 8 of The California Tenants' Handbook, Moskovitz, Warner and Sherman, Nolo Press (see back of this book for order information).

Your Honor, I have brought along Clem Houndstooth as
a witness. Mr. Houndstooth is the tenant who moved
in three days after Mr. Andrews moved out. Inciden-
tally, your Honor, the place was so dirty that I only
charged Mr. Houndstooth a $200 cleaning deposit,
because he agreed to clean it up himself."

Judge: (looking at Clem Houndstooth) "Do you
wish to say something?"

Clem Houndstooth: (standing) "Yes, I do. Mr.
Robertson asked me to come down and back him up and I
am glad to do it because I put in two full days
cleaning that place up. I like a clean house, your
Honor, not a half-way clean, half-way dirty house. I
just don't think that a house is clean if the oven is
full of gunk, there is mold in the bathroom, and the
insides of the cupboards are grimy. All these conditions existed at 1611 Spruce St. when I moved in.
I just don't believe that anyone could think that
that place was clean."

Judge: "Mr. Andrews, do you have anything to
add?"

John Andrews: (standing up) "Yes, I sure do.
First, as to the mildew problem. The house is forty
years old and there is some dampness in the wall of
the bathroom. Maybe there is a leaky pipe someplace
behind the tile. I cleaned it a number of times, but
it always came back. I talked to Mr. Fisk in Mr.
Robertson's office about the problem about a month
after I moved in and he told me that I would have to
do the best I could because they couldn't afford to
tear the wall apart. As to the cupboards and stove,
they are both old. The cabinets haven't been painted
in ten years, so, of course, they aren't perfect, and
that old stove was a lot dirtier when I moved in than
it is now."

Judge: "What about the refrigerator, Mr.
Andrews? Was that defrosted?"

John Andrews: "No, your Honor, it wasn't, but
it had been defrosted about three weeks before I
moved out and I thought that it was good enough the
way it was."

Judge: "O.K., if no one else has anything to add, I want to return your pictures and letters. You will receive my decision by mail in a few days."

Now, I have a little surprise for you. This was a real case taking place not in Fresno in 198_, but in Small Claims Court in San Francisco on September 14, 1977. As they used to say on "Dragnet," "Only the names have been changed to protect the innocent." And I have another surprise for you. I spoke to the judge after the court session and I know how the case came out. The judge explained his reasoning to me as follows.

"This is a typical case in which both sides have some right on their side. What is clean to one person may be dirty to another. Based on what I heard, I would have to guess that the old tenant made a fairly conscientious effort to clean up and probably left the place about as clean as it was when he moved in, but that the new tenant, Houndstooth, had much higher standards and convinced the landlord that it was filthy. The landlord may not have needed too much convincing since he probably would just as well keep the deposit. But I did hear enough to convince

141

me that Andrews, the old tenant, didn't do a perfect job cleaning up. My decision will be that Andrews gets a judgment for the return of $250 of the $400 deposit, with no punitive damages. I believe that $150 is more than enough to compensate the landlord for any damages he suffered."

I then asked the judge if he felt that the case was well presented. He replied substantially as follows:

"Better than average. I think I got a pretty good idea of what the problems were. The witnesses were helpful and the pictures gave me an idea that the place wasn't a total mess. Both sides could have done better, however. Andrews could have had a witness to talk about the condition when he moved in if it was truly dirtier than when he left. Another witness to testify to the apartment's cleanliness when he moved out would have been good too. His friend, Carol Spann, seemed to be a very close friend and I wasn't sure that she was objective when it came to judging whether the place was clean. The landlord, Robertson, could also have done better. He could have presented a more disinterested witness, although I must say that Houndstooth's testimony was pretty convincing. Also he could have had pictures documenting the dirty conditions and an estimate from a cleaning company for how much they would have charged to clean the mess up. Without going to too much trouble, I think that either side could have probably done somewhat better with more thorough preparation."

C. Don't Forget To Ask For Your Costs

When you finish your presentation to the judge, you should be sure he realizes that you have incurred certain costs. These can be added to the judgment amount. As we have mentioned, you can't recover for such things as time off from work, paying a baby-sitter or xerox charges. You can recover for:

* Your filing fee

*   Service of process

*   Subpoenaed witness fees [3]

*   Cost of necessary documents, such as verification of car ownership by the D.M.V.

If you forget to get your costs added to the judgment in court and want to go to the trouble, you can file a "Memorandum of Costs" with the Small Claims clerk within five days after judgment. Forms are available at the clerk's office. For information on recovering costs incurred after judgment when your opponent won't voluntarily pay the judgment, see Chapter 24 C.

---

[3] Fees must be approved by the judge. Fees for subpoenaing witnesses and documents are only likely to be approved if absolutely necessary.

16.

Motor Vehicle Repair Cases

Most Small Claims Court cases fall into a dozen
or so broad categories with perhaps another dozen
sub-categories. In the next six chapters, we look at
the most common types of cases and discuss strategies
to handle each. Even if your fact situation doesn't
fit neatly in one of these categories, read them all.
By taking a few hints here and a little information
there, you should be able to piece together a good
plan of action. For example, suggestions I make to
handle motor vehicle repair disputes can easily be
applied to cases involving major appliances such as
televisions, washers, expensive stereos, etc.

Let's start by imagining that you go to the auto
repair shop to pick up your trusty, but slightly
greying, steed. The bill is $725 for a complete
engine overhaul. This seems a little steep, but
after the mechanic tells you all about the great job
he did, and you remember that inflation is a fact of
life, you drive out of the garage in something

approaching a cheerful mood. One of life's little
hassles has been taken care of, at least temporarily.

You're right--temporarily can sometimes be a
very short time. In this case, it lasts only until
you head up the first hill. What's that funny noise,
you think? Why don't I have more power? Oh shit,
you say (you never swear, but there are some extreme
provocations where nothing else will do). You turn
around and drive back to the garage. Not only are
you out $725, but your car works worse than it did
when you brought it in.

Funny, no one seems as pleasant as they did
before. Funny, no one seems to have time to listen
to you. Finally, after several explanations and a
bit of foot stomping, you get someone to say that
they will look the car over again. You take a bus
home, trying not to be paranoid. Two days later, you
call. Nothing has been done. You yell at the garage
owner and then call your bank to stop payment on the
check. You are told that they cashed it yesterday.
Another few days pass and the garage tells you that
the problem is in a part of the engine that they
didn't work on. You only paid for a "short block
job" they keep telling you. "Give us another $300
and we can surely solve this new problem," they add.

In disgust, you go down and pick up your
crippled friend and drive it home--very, very slowly.
You are furious and decide to pursue every legal
remedy, no matter what the trouble. How do you
start?

First, park your car, take a shower and have a
glass of wine. Nothing gets decided well when you're
mad. Now, going back to the reasoning we used at the
beginning of this book, ask yourself some basic
questions:

A. Have I Suffered A Loss?

That's easy. Your car doesn't work, you paid
out a lot of money and the garage wants another bun-
dle to fix it. Clearly, you have suffered a loss.

B. Did The Negligence Of The Garage Cause My Loss?

Ah ha, now we get to the nitty gritty. In this type of case you can almost always expect the garage to claim that they did their work properly and that the car simply needs more work. Maybe the garage is right--it's your job to prove that they aren't. Doing so will make your case; failing to do so will break it. You better get to work.

Step 1   Collect Available Evidence

First, get all evidence together where time is of the essence. In this fact situation, this means getting your used parts (it's a good idea to do this anytime you have major work done.)[1] If the garage will not give them to you, make your request by letter, keeping a copy for your file. If you get the parts, fine--if you don't, you have evidence that the garage is badly run or has something to hide.

Step 2   Have The Car Checked

Before you drive many miles, have your car checked by an established local mechanic or mechanics. Often it is possible to get free estimates from repair shops. But be sure that at least one of the people who looks the car over is willing to come with you to Small Claims Court if the need arises.

Step 3   Try To Settle Your Case

By now you should have a pretty good idea as to what the first garage did wrong. Call them and ask that either the job be redone, or that they give you a refund of part or all of your money. Often the

---

1 In California you are entitled to get your parts back by law, just as you are entitled to a written estimate before repairs are made. See the Compleat California Consumer Catalogue, available from the California Department of Consumer Affairs, 1020 N St., Sacramento, CA 95814.

repair shop will agree to do some, or all, of the
work over to avoid a further hassle. If they agree
to take the car back, try to get a written agreement
detailing what they will do and how long it will
take. Also, talk to the mechanic who will actually
work on the car to be sure he understands what needs
to be done.

Step 4   Write A Demand Letter

If the garage isn't cooperative, it's time to
write them a formal demand letter. Remember our
discussion in Chapter 6. Your letter should be
short, polite and written with an eye to a judge
reading it. In this situation you could write
something like this:

                                        Haig Mackey
                                        15 Orange St.
                                        Laguna Beach, CA
Happy Days Motors
100 Speedway
Corona Del Mar, CA

Dear People:

On August 13, 198-, I brought my 1972 Dodge to your garage. You
agreed to do a complete engine rebuild job for $725. You told me,
"Your car will be running like a watch when we're through with it."
The car worked well when I brought it in, but was a little short on
power. Two days later when I picked up my car, it barely moved at
all. The engine made such a clanging noise that I have been afraid
to drive it.

I have repeatedly asked you to fix the car or to refund my money.
You have refused. Shortly after the work was done, I also asked for
my used parts to be returned. You refused to give them to me even
though this is a violation of state law.

I have had several mechanics look my car over since you worked
on it. They all agree that you did your job improperly and even
installed some used parts that came from a 1974 Plymouth. The
work you did on the engine rings was particularly badly done.

After receiving no response from you, I had the work re-done at a
cost of $610. My car now works well. Please refund my $725. Should
you fail to do so, I will exhaust all my legal remedies including
complaining to interested state and local agencies and taking this
dispute to Small Claims Court.

May I hear from you promptly.

                                        Haig Mackey

cc: California Dept. of Consumer Affairs
     Bureau of Automotive Repair
     3116 Bradshaw Road
     Sacramento, CA

: Most small independent garages don't make
any written warranty or guarantee of their work.
However, if you were given any promises in writing,
mention them here in your letter.

Step 5   File Your Court Papers

If you still get no satisfactory response from
the garage, file your papers at the Small Claims
clerk's office of your local Small Claims Court.
Re-read Chapters 7-10.

Step 6   Prepare For Court

If you want a third person (a judge) to
understand your case, you must understand it
yourself. Sounds simple, doesn't it? It does to me
too until I get involved with machinery. My opinion
of cars (and most other machinery) is low--they are
supposed to work without trouble, but most of us know
better.

For me to argue a case in Small Claims such as
the one we are talking about here could be a disaster
unless I did some homework. This sort of disaster is
repeated often in Small Claims. I have seen many,
many people argue cases about their cars knowing no
more than "the car was supposed to be fixed, your
Honor, and it's worse than ever." On some mornings
when the roses are in bloom, the peaches are sweet
and the angels are in heaven, this is enough to win
--usually it isn't. Why? Because the people from
the garage are likely to have a terrific sounding
story about the wonderful job they did. They will
talk about pistons, rings, bearings, pulling the head
and turning the cam shaft. It's all likely to sound
so impressive that you can easily find yourself on
the defensive.

This sort of thing needn't happen if you are
willing to learn a little about your car (or whatever
machinery is involved). Fifteen minutes' conversation
with a knowledgeable mechanic may be all you need to
understand what's going on. Also, your local library

will have manuals about every type of car, complete
with diagrams, etc.

    REMEMBER THE JUDGE: In Chapter 13 I mentioned
that it's important to pay attention to whom you are
presenting your case. Most Small Claims judges don't
understand the insides of cars any better than you
do. People often become lawyers because they don't
like to get their hands dirty. So be prepared to
deal with a person who nods his head but doesn't
really understand the difference between the drive
shaft and the axle. Car cases are often easier to
present to a woman judge. Women don't usually have
the same ego involvement with cars that men do. They
are more willing to say "I don't know."

Step 7 Appearing In Court

    When you appear in court, be sure that you are
well organized. Bring all the letters you have
written, or received, about your car problem as well
as written warranties (if any), photographs if they
are helpful and your used parts if they aid in making
your case. Several times in cases involving
machinery, I have seen people give effective
testimony by presenting a large drawing illustrating
the screw-up. Also, be sure that you get your
witnesses to the courtroom on time. The best way to
do this is to pick them up at home or work and
personally escort them.

    If you are well prepared you should win the sort
of case outlined here without difficulty. Judges
drive cars and have to get them fixed; they tend to
be sympathetic with this type of consumer complaint.
Simply present your story (see Chapter 15), your
documentation and your witnesses. If you feel that
your opponent is snowing the judge with a lot of
technical lingo, get his (her) Honor back on the
track by asking that the technical terms be explained
in ordinary English. This will be a relief to
everyone in the courtroom except your opponent. You
will likely find that, once his case is shorn of all
the magic words, it will shrink from tiger to
pussycat.

17.

Motor Vehicle Purchase Cases

All too often someone buys a motor vehicle, drives it a short way, and watches it fall apart. All too often the seller won't stand behind the product sold or work out some sort of fair adjustment. There are major differences in approach between buying a new vehicle from a dealer, buying a used vehicle from a dealer and buying a used vehicle from a private party. Let's look at each situation individually.

A. New Vehicles

Here the most common problem is the lemon with major manufacturing defects. Before considering Small Claims Court, California consumers should fully understand the terms of Civil Code Section 1793.2 (the lemon law). The law provides that if within one year or 12,000 miles the same noncomformity has been subject to repair four or more times by the manufacturer or its agents for a cumulative total of more than 30 calendar days, the manufacturer must either replace the goods or reimburse the buyer.

If, as part of the repair process, a dispute
arises, it must first be submitted to a "qualified
third party dispute resolution process if one exists"
(see Civil Code 1793.2(e)(3) for details). This
would normally be an independent arbitration program
run by the Better Business Bureau or some similar
organization.[1] If the buyer is not satisfied with
this decision, s/he may then take the case to court.
The decision of the third party arbitrator shall be
admissible in court, however.

Unfortunately, many disputes involving new
vehicles don't fall under the lemon law. This would
be the situation if the same defect didn't reoccur
four times or if problems develop just after the
warranty expires.

Sometimes it seems as though there is a little
destruct switch set to flip fifteen minutes after you
hit "one year or twelve thousand miles, whichever
comes first." Often too, a problem starts to surface
while the car is still under warranty and a dealer
makes inadequate repairs which last scarcely longer
than the remainder of the warranty term. When the
same problem develops again after the warranty has
run out, the dealer refuses to fix it.

Just the other day I saw a case involving this
sort of problem. A man with a new, expensive
European car sued the local dealer and the parent car
company's West Coast representative. He claimed that
he had repeatedly brought the car into the dealer's
repair shop with transmission problems while it was
still under warranty. Each time adjustments were
made which seemed to eliminate the problem. But each
time, after a month or so, the same problem would
reappear. A few months after the warranty ran out,
the transmission died. Even though the car was only
a little over a year old, and had gone less than
20,000 miles, both the dealer and the parent car
company refused to repair it. Their refusals continued even though the owner repeatedly wrote them,
demanding action.

---

1 The automobile companies have worked out arbitration arrangements
that seem to be reasonably fair.

How did the car owner go about dealing with his problem? First, because he needed his car, he went ahead and had the repairs made. This involved a cost in excess of $1,500, the Small Claims limit. Then, he filed his Small Claims action. Because the dealer was located in the same city as he was, the man could sue locally.[2] In this situation it would have been adequate to sue only the local dealer and not the West Coast representative of the car company, but it didn't hurt to sue both following the general rule, "when in doubt, sue all possible defendants."

In court, the car owner was well prepared and had a reasonably easy time. Both he and his wife testified as to their trials and tribulations with the car. They gave the judge copies of the several letters they had written the dealer, one of which listed by date the fifteen times they had taken the car to the dealer's shop. They also produced a letter from the owner of the independent garage which finally fixed the transmission stating that, when he took the transmission apart, he discovered a defect in its original assembly. The new car dealer simply testified that his mechanics had done their best to fix the car under the warranty. He then pointed out that, once the warranty had run out, he was no longer responsible. The dealer made no effort to challenge the car owner's story, nor did he bring his own mechanics to testify as to what they had done while the car was still under warranty. The car owner won. He presented a convincing case to the point that the defect had never been fixed when it should have been under the warranty. The dealer did nothing to rebut it. As the judge noted to me after the hearing, an $18,000 car should come with a transmission that will last longer than 20,000 miles. The car owner would have had an even stronger case if he had brought the independent garage man to court, but the letters, along with his own testimony and that of his wife, were adequate in a situation where the dealer didn't put up much of a defense.

---

2 Only one defendant need be local to sue in a particular judicial district. The fact that the car company's West Coast headquarters was in a different part of the state didn't cause a problem with bringing the suit where the dealer was located (see Chapter 9).

NOTE: In this sort of case it is very convincing to have documentation of all the trips you
have made to the dealer's repair shop. You may be
able to find copies of work orders you signed, or
cancelled checks if you were charged. If you don't
have this sort of record, sit down with a calendar
and do your best to make an accurate list. Give the
list to the judge in court. He will accept it as
true unless the car dealer disputes it.

Even if your car is no longer covered by a
written warranty when trouble develops, you may have
a case. There are general common law concepts of
warranty that give you protection over and above the
actual written paper that comes with the vehicle.
Thus, if the engine on your properly maintained car
burns out after 25,000 miles, you will stand a good
chance of recovering some money even though the
written warranty has expired. Engines are simply
supposed to last longer than 25,000 miles. You may
also wish to consider other remedies in addition to
Small Claims Court such as trying to enlist the help
of state regulatory agencies.[3] One strategy of last
resort if you don't have much equity in the car is to
simply drive it to the dealer and leave it there,
refusing to make any more payments until it is fixed.
This is an extreme remedy and should only be con-
sidered in an extreme situation. It does have the
beauty of shifting the responsibility to take action,
legal or otherwise, to the other side. If you do
this, be sure to set forth in writing all the circumstances surrounding the mechanical deficiencies
and your efforts to remedy the situation, and send a
copy to both the car dealer and the bank or other
financial institution that has the loan.

B. Used Vehicle Dealers

Recovering from used vehicle dealers can be
tricky for several reasons. Unlike new vehicle
dealers who are usually somewhat dependent upon their
reputation in the community for honesty, used vehicle
dealers commonly have no positive reputation to start

---

3 Again I recommend the Compleat California Consumer Catalogue published by the State of California.

with and survive by becoming experts at self-protection. Also (and don't underestimate this one), judges almost never buy used vehicles and therefore aren't normally as sympathetic to the problems used vehicle owners encounter. Chances are a judge has had a problem getting his (her) new car fixed under a warranty, but has never bought a ten-year-old Plymouth in "tip-top shape," only to have it die two blocks after leaving Honest Al's.

The principal self-protection device employed by used vehicle dealers is the "as is" designation in the written sales contract. The salesperson may promise the moon, but when you read the fine print of the contract, you will see it clearly stated that the seller takes absolutely no responsibility for the condition of the vehicle.

Time and again I have sat in court and heard hard luck stories like this:

"I bought the car for $1,200 two months ago. The man at 'Lucky Larry's' told me that it had a completely reconditioned engine and transmission. I drove the car less than 400 miles and it died. I mean really died--it didn't roll over and dig itself a hole, but it may as well have. I had it towed to an independent garage and they told me that, as far as they could see, no engine or transmission work had ever been done. They estimated that to put the car right would cost $800. I got one more estimate which was even higher, so I borrowed the $800 and had the work done. I feel I really got took by Lucky Larry. I have with me the cancelled check for the $800 in repairs, plus the mechanic who did the work who can testify as to the condition of the car when he saw it."

Unfortunately, this plaintiff will probably lose. Why? Because going back to the sort of issues that we discussed in Chapter 2, he has proven only half of his case. He has shown his loss (he bought a $1,200 car that wasn't worth $1,200), but he has not dealt with the issue of the defendant's responsibility to make the loss good ("liability"). Almost surely the used car dealer will testify that he "had no way of knowing how long a ten-year-old Plymouth would last and that, for this very reason, sold the car "as is." He will then show the judge a written contract that not only has the "as is" designation, but which will say someplace in the fine print that "this written contract is the entire agreement between the parties and that no oral statements or representations made by the dealer or any salesperson are part of the contract."

How can you fight this sort of cynical semi-fraud? It's difficult to do so after the fact. The time for self-protection is before you buy a vehicle when you can have it checked by an expert and can insist that any promises made by the salesperson as to the condition of the car or the availability of repairs, be put in writing. Of course, good advice such as this, after the damage has been done, "isn't worth more than a passle of warm spit" as former Vice-President John Nance Garner so graphically put it. If you have just been cheated on a used car deal, you want to know what, if anything, you can do now. Here are some suggestions.

1. If the car broke almost immediately after you took it out of the used car lot, you can file in Small Claims and argue that you were defrauded. Your theory is that, no matter what the written contract said, there was also an implied warranty that you purchased a car, not a junk heap. When the dealer produces his "as is" contract, argue that it is no defense to fraud.

2. You may want to consider having the car towed back to the lot and refusing to make future payments. This puts the burden on the bank or finance company to sue you, at which point you can defend on the basis of fraud. If you take this approach, be sure you have excellent documentation that the car was truly a lemon. Of course, you will probably have made some down payment, so even in this situation you may wish to initiate action in Small Claims Court.

3. Have your car checked over by someone who knows cars and would be willing to testify if need be. If this person can find affirmative evidence that you were cheated, you will greatly improve your Small Claims case. They might, for example, find that the speedometer had been tampered with in violation of state law, or that a heavy grade of truck oil had been put in the crank case so that the car wouldn't belch smoke. Also, this is the sort of case where a Subpoena Duces Tecum (subpoena for documents) might be of help (see Chapter 13). You might wish to subpoena records the car dealer has pertaining to his purchase price of the car, or its condition when purchased. It might also be helpful to learn the name of the car's former owner with the idea of contacting him or her. With a little digging you may be able to develop information that will enable you to convince a judge that you have been defrauded.

4. Consider other remedies besides Small Claims Court. These can include checking with your state Department of Consumer Affairs, or the local Department of Motor Vehicles to see if used car lots are regulated. In California and many other states, the Department of Motor Vehicles licenses used car dealers and can be very helpful in getting disputes

resolved, particularly where your complaint is one of many against the sale dealer for similar practices. Also, contact your local District Attorney's office. Most now have a consumer fraud division which can be of great help. If you can convince them that what happened to you smells rotten, or your complaint happens to be against someone they have already identified as a borderline criminal, they will likely call the used car dealer in for a chat. In theory, the D.A.'s only job is to bring a criminal action which will be of no direct aid in getting your money back, but in practice, negotiations often go on which can result in restitution. In plain words, this means that the car dealer will be told, "Look buddy, you're right on the edge of the law here (or maybe over the edge). If you clean up your act, which means taking care of all complaints against you and seeing that there are no more, we will close your file. If you don't, I suggest you hire a good lawyer because you're going to need one."

C. Used Vehicles From Private Parties

Normally it is easier to win a case against a private party than it is a used vehicle dealer. This runs counter to both common sense and fairness, as a private party is likely to be more honest than a dealer. But fair or not, the fact is that a non-dealer is usually less sophisticated in self-protection than is a pro. Indeed, in most private party sales the seller does no more than sign over the title slip in exchange for the agreed upon price. No formal contract is signed that says the buyer takes the car "as is."

If trouble develops soon after you purchase the vehicle and you are out money for unexpectd repairs, you may be able to recover. Again, the problem is usually not proving your loss, but convincing the judge that the seller of the vehicle is responsible ("liable") to make your loss good. To do this, you normally must prove that the seller represented the vehicle to be in better shape than in fact it was, and that you relied on these promises when you made the deal.

Recently, I watched Barbara, a twenty-year-old college student, succeed in proving just such a case. She sued John for $900, claiming that the B.M.W. motorcycle she purchased from him was in far worse shape than he had advertised. In court, she ably and convincingly outlined her conversations with John around the purchase of the motorycle, testifying that he repeatedly told her that the cycle was "hardly used." She hadn't gotten any of his promises in writing, but she did a creative job of developing and presenting what evidence she had. This included:

A copy of her letter to John which clearly outlined her position.

---

14 Stockton St.
Corte Madera, Calif.

January 27, 19___

John Malinosky
321 South Zaporah
Albany, Calif.

Dear Mr. Malinosky:

This letter is a follow-up to our recent phone conversation in which you refused to discuss the fact that the 19___ B.M.W. motorcycle I purchased from you on January 15 is not in the "excellent condition" that you claimed.

To review: on January 12 I saw your ad for a motorcycle that was "almost new - hardly used - excellent condition" in the local flea market newspaper. I called you and you told me that the cycle was a terrific bargain and that you would never sell it except that you needed money for school. I told you that I didn't know much about machinery.

The next day you took me for a ride on the cycle. You told me specifically that:

1. The cycle had just been tuned up.
2. The cycle had been driven less than 10,000 miles.
3. The cycle had never been raced or used roughly.
4. That if anything went wrong with the cycle in the next month or two, you would see that it was fixed.

I didn't have the cycle more than a week when the brakes went out. When I had them checked, the mechanic told me that the carburetor also needed work (I confirmed this with another mechanic - see attached estimate). The mechanics also told me that the cycle had been driven at least 50,000 miles (perhaps a lot more) and that it needed a tune-up. In addition they showed me caked mud and scratches unddr the cycle which indicated to them that it had been driven extensively off the road in rough terrain and had probably been raced on dirt tracks.

The low mechanic's estimate to do the repairs was $900. Before having the work done, I called you to explain the situation and to give you a chance to arrange for the repairs to be made, or to make them yourself. You laughed at me and said,"Sister, do what you need to do - you're not getting dime one from me."

Again I respectfully request that you make good on the promises you made to me on January 15. I enclose a copy of the mechanic's bill for $900 along with several higher estimates that I received from other repair shops.

Sincerely,

Barbara Parker

Copies of repair bills (and estimates) dated within two weeks of her purchase of the cycle, the lowest of which came to $900.

A copy of John's newspaper ad which she answered. It read: "B.M.W. 500 c.c., almost new—hardly used—excellent condition—$1,500."

Finally, Barbara presented the judge with this note from the mechanic who fixed the cycle.

To Whom It May Concern:

It's hard for me to get off work but if you need me, please ask the judge to delay the case a few days. All I have to say is this: the B.M.W. that Barbara Parker brought to me was in fair shape. It's impossible to be exact, but I guess that it had been driven at least 50,000-75,000 miles and I can say for sure that it was driven a lot of miles on dirt.

Respectfully submitted,

Al "Honker" Green
February 3, 19___

Barbara quickly outlined the whole story for the judge and emphasized that she had saved for six months to get the money to make the purchase.[4]

Next, John had his turn. He helped Barbara make her case by acting like a weasel. His testimony consisted mostly of a lot of vague philosophy about machinery. He kept asking "how could I know just when it would break?" When the judge asked him specific questions about the age, condition and previous history of the cycle, he clammed up as if he was a mafioso called to testify by a Senate anti-racketeering committee. Finally, the judge in frustration asked John if he had anything concrete to

---

4 This sort of testimony isn't relevant, but it never hurts. As an old appeals court judge who had seen at least 75 summers told me when I graduated from law school and was proud of my technical mastery of the law, "Son, don't worry about the law—just convince the judge that truth and virtue are on your side and he will always find some technicality to support you." No one ever gave me better advice.

say. John said yes and started explaining how when
you sell things, you "puff them up a little" and that
"women shouldn't be allowed to drive motorcycles
anyway." Finally, the judge asked him to please sit
down.

IMPORTANT: In this type of case, it's often one
person's word against another's. Any shred of tan-
gible evidence for either side can be enough to shift
the balance to that side. Of course, if you have a
friend who witnessed or heard any part of the transaction, his or her testimony will be extremely
valuable. Getting a mechanic to check over a vehicle
and then testify for you is also a good strategy.
Sometimes you can get some help from the small blue
book that lists wholesale and retail prices for used
cars. Several times I have seen people bring this
book (libraries and car dealers have them) into court
and show the judge that they paid above the Blue Book
price for a used car "because the car was represented
to be in extra good shape." This doesn't constitute
much in the way of real proof that you were ripped
off, but it is helpful to at least show the judge
that you paid a premium price for unsound goods.

18.
Cases Where
Money Is Owed

A. From The Creditor's Point Of View

The job of the plaintiff in a case where he or she is suing for non-payment of a debt is to prove that a valid debt exists and that it has not been paid. Here are a few suggestions.

1. Sue Promptly

When you are owed money, be sure you sue promptly. You will find a discussion of the Statutes of Limitations applicable to different sorts of debts in Chapter 5. But even when there is no danger that the limitation period will run out, it makes sense to proceed as soon as reasonably possible. Judges just aren't as sympathetic to old claims. Several times when I have sat as judge, I have wondered why someone waited three years to sue for $500. Was it because he/she wasn't honestly convinced that his/her suit was valid? Another reason to sue right away is that you will get your money faster. You will be pleasantly surprised that a fair number of people will pay up without the need of your going to court.

2. Written Contracts

If the debt is based on a written contract, be
sure that your paperwork is in order. Bring to court
the original copy of any written note proving the
indebtedness so that the court can cancel it when the
judgment is entered. Also bring any ledger sheets or
other documentation as to any payments made, interest
charged, etc. Often I have seen otherwise sensible
looking business people show up with botched records
and become flustered when closely questioned by the
judge. The courtroom is not the place to straighten
out a poor accounting system.

NOTE: If you provide goods or services it's
wise to include in all letters and bills to the debtor a request that they notify you if the goods were
defective, or the services substandard. Bring copies
of these notices to court. If the debtor shows up
with a story about not paying because of some problem
or defect, produce your documents. The fact that you
requested this sort of information long ago and that
no complaints were made previous to your court
hearing will pretty clearly imply that the defendant
is fabricating his current complaint.

3. Oral Contracts

A debt based on an oral contract is legal as
long as the contract could have been carried out in
one year. However, you may face a problem proving
that the debt exists if the defendant denies that he
borrowed the money, or bought the goods. Your best
bet is to come up with some written documentation
that your version of the story is true. If you have
no written evidence (cancelled checks, letters or
notes asking for more time to pay, etc.), your next
step is to try to think of any person who knows about
the debt and who would be willing to testify. For
example, if you asked the defendant to pay you and he
said in the presence of your friend, "I'll pay you
next month," or "You will never get your money back,"
or anything to indicate that a loan existed, bring
your friend as a witness.

4. Proving Your Case

All too often a business will send the same bookkeeper-type of court for every case. He or she will be competent enough in establishing that the books say that the money is owed, but will be helpless if the defendant starts raising questions about anything else. For example, if you own a T.V. repair business and are suing on an unpaid repair bill in a situation where the defendant claims that you did lousy work, you will want someone in court who knows the details of the job. If you are incorporated, you can authorize the person who actually did the work to appear without the necessity of going yourself. As noted in Chapter 7, both incorporated and unincorporated businesses can send employees to represent them in court on claims involving unpaid bills, but in a case involving whether T.V. repairs were made, the owner of an unincorporated business would have to show up himself. Of course, he or she could bring the person who actually did the work as a witness. If you find yourself in court suing on a debt when you suddenly realize that you don't have the right witness in court, ask that the case be delayed a few days. Many judges will do this if they feel that you made a sincere effort to be ready, but something came up that you couldn't foresee.

NOTE: Many businesses, and especially professionals such as doctors, dentists and lawyers, don't use Small Claims Court to collect unpaid bills because they think it takes too much of their own time, or is "undignified." You will have to worry about your "dignity" yourself, but I can tell you that Small Claims Court actions can be handled with very little time and expense once you get the hang of it. This is especially true when you consider that the alternative is to turn the bill over to a collection agency or not to collect it at all. As long as the suit simply involves getting a judgment for an unpaid bill, you can send your bookkeeper to court. Wait until you have several cases and schedule them on the same day. You will find that, once your bookkeeper understands the system, he or she can often be in and out in fifteen minutes to a half hour. Once you get your judgment, your secretarial staff should be able to handle the collection activities described in Chapter 24.

B. From The Debtor's Point Of View

While there is an increasing number of private individuals using Small Claims Court, most plaintiffs trying to collect money are businesses or government entities, such as a library, hospital or city tax office. Debt case defendants are often individuals with little in their pockets but holes. Not many years ago, debt collection cases so numerically dominated Small Claims Court dockets that the court was in danger of becoming a "bill collectors' court." For a variety of reasons, perhaps the most important being the hopelessness of getting disputes resolved in more formal courts, Small Claims Courts have recently been used by a much wider variety of people to settle a broader range of disputes. This has been a healthy development and now the representatives of the department stores, tire companies and credit jewelers are only part of the crowd.

When I first watched debt collection cases, I did so with scant attention. I assumed that individuals being pursued by large institutions were bound to lose, especially since they mostly did owe the money. I even wondered why a lot of folks bothered to show up--knowing in advance that they had no defense, and no money. I thought it unjust that our society divided its bounty so unfairly and sad that the poor had no better defense than their inability to pay. But then a curious thing happened. Many of the "downtrodden" I had dismissed so easily refused to play their docile parts. Instead of shuffling in with heads down and nothing constructive to say, they argued back, stamped their feet and acted like the proud and dignified people they were. I realized suddenly that I was the only person in the courtroom that had dismissed them. I learned that morning, and on dozens of later mornings, that there are lots of ways to constructively defend non-payment of debt cases. Here are some examples.

A local hospital sued an unemployed man for failure to pay an emergency room bill for $278. It seemed an open and shut case--the person from the hospital had all the proper records, and the defendant hadn't paid. Then the defendant told his side of it. He was taken to the emergency room suffering from a gunshot wound. Because it was a busy night and he was not about to die, he was kept waiting four hours for treatment. When treatment was given, it was minimal and he suffered later complications that might have been avoided if he had been treated promptly. He said he didn't mind paying a fair amount, but that he didn't feel he got $278 worth of care for seeing a doctor for half an hour. The judge agreed and gave judgment to the hospital for $90, plus court and service of process costs. After the defendant explained that he had only his unemployment check, the judge ordered that he be allowed to pay off the judgment at the rate of $10 per month.

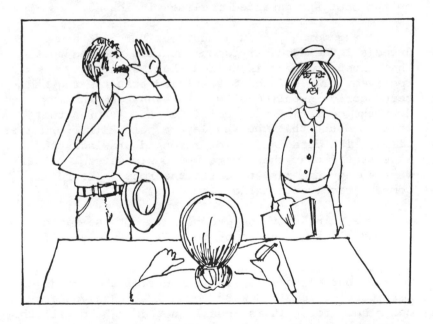

A large tire company sued a woman for not paying the balance on a tire bill. She had purchased eight tires for two pickup trucks and still owed $312.50. The tire company properly presented the judge with the original copy of a written contract along with the woman's payment record, and then waited for judgment. They are still waiting. The woman, who ran a small neighborhood gardening and landscaping business, produced several advertising flyers from the tire company which strongly implied, but didn't quite state, that the tires would last at least 40,000 miles. She then testified and presented a witness to the fact that the tires had only gone 25,000 miles before wearing out. The defendant also had copies of four letters written over the past year to the head-quarters of the tire company in the Midwest com-plaining about the tires. Both in the letters, and in court, she repeatedly stated that the salesperson at the tire company told her several times that the tires were guaranteed for 40,000 miles. Putting this all together, the judge declared the tires should be prorated on the basis of 40,000 miles and gave the tire company a judgment for only $102, instead of the $312.50 requested. The woman wrote them out a check on the spot and departed feeling vindicated.

A rug company sued a customer for $686 and pro-duced all the necessary documentation showing that the carpet had been installed, but no payment received. The defendant testified that the rug had been poorly installed with an uneven seam running down the center of the room. He had pictures that left no doubt that the rug layers were either drunk or blind. The defendant also presented drawings that illustrated that there were obviously several better ways to cut the carpet to fit the room. The rug company received nothing.

The point of these examples is not the facts of the individual situations--yours will surely differ. The point is that there are all sorts of defenses, and partial defenses, and that it makes good sense to defend yourself creatively if you feel that goods or services you received were worth less than you are being sued for. It is usually not enough to tell the judge that you were dissatisfied with what you received. A little more imagination is required. If shoddy goods are involved, show them to the judge. If you received bad service, bring a witnesss or other supporting evidence. If, for example, you got roof repairs done that resulted in more holes than you had before, take pictures of the rain leaking in, and get an estimate from another roofer.

There is often a tactical advantage for the debtor in the fact that the person who appears in court on behalf of the creditor is not the same person that he had dealings with. If, for example, you state that a salesperson told you X, Y and Z, that person probably won't be present to state otherwise. This may till a closely balanced case to you. It is not inappropriate for you to point out to the judge that your opponent has only books and ledgers and no first hand knowledge of the situation. The judge may sometimes continue the case until another day to allow the creditor to have whatever employee(s) you dealt with present, but often this is impossible because the employee in question will have left the job, or be otherwise unavailable.

A LITTLE MORE TIME TO PAY: In California (Code of Civil Procedure 117) and in many other states, the judge has considerable discretion to order that a judgment be paid in installments. Thus, a judge could find that you owe the phone company $200, but allow you to pay it off at $20 per month, instead of all at once. Time payments can be particularly helpful if you don't have the money to pay all at once, but fear a wage attachment or other collection activity by the creditor. Don't be afraid to ask the judge for time payments--he or she won't know that you want them if you don't. People who owe money and want to learn more about their legal rights in such areas as attachments, bankruptcy, dealing with collection agencies, etc., should see Nolo Press' California Debtors' Handbook--Billpayers' Rights Honigsberg and Warner (order information in back of book).

19.

Vehicle Accident Cases

It is a rare Small Claims session that does not include at least one fender bender. Usually these cases are badly prepared and presented. The judge commonly makes a decision at least partially by guess. I know from personal experience that it sometimes wouldn't take much additional evidence for me to completely reverse a decision. In Chapter 2, I discuss the concept of negligence and what's involved in proving it. Re-read this chapter before proceeding.

The average vehicle accident that ends up in Small Claims Court doesn't involve personal injury, but is concerned with damage to one, or both, parties' car, cycle, R.V., moped or whatever.[1] Because of some quirk of character that seems to be deeply embedded in our overgrown monkey brains, it is almost impossible for most of us to admit that we are bad drivers, or are at fault in a car accident. We will cheerfully acknowledge that we aren't terrific looking or geniuses, but we all believe that we drive like angels. Out of fantasies such as these lawsuits are made.

---

[1] Cases involving all but the most minor personal injuries don't belong in Small Claims Court as they will result in settlements of more than the Small Claims maximum.

A. Who Can Sue Whom?

The owner of a vehicle must sue for damage to
the vehicle, even if he wasn't driving when the damage occurred. Any person injured, whether driver,
passenger, or pedestrian, must sue for his or her own
personal injuries. Suit should be brought against
the negligent driver and, if the driver is not the
registered owner of the car, the registered owner,
too. Both the driver and the registered owner are
liable. To find out who owns a car, contact the
Department of Motor Vehicles. As long as you can
tell them the license number, they can tell you the
registered owner.

Be particularly wary when you are opposing a bus
or truck driver. Many of these people suffer problems on their jobs if they are found to be at fault
in too many accidents. As a result, they deny fault
almost automatically. Judges usually know this and
are often unsympathetic when a bus driver says that
there has never been a time when he "didn't look both
ways twice, count to ten and say the Lord's Prayer"
before pulling out from a bus stop. Still, it never
hurts to question the driver in court as to whether
his company has any demerit system or other penalty
for being at fault in an accident.

B. Was There a Witness To The Accident?

Because the judge has no way of knowing what
happened unless one or more people tell him (her), a
good witness can make or break your case. It is
better to have a disinterested witness than a close
friend or family member, but any witness is better
than no witness. If the other guy is likely to have
a witness and you have none, you will have to work
extra hard to develop other evidence to overcome this
advantage. Re-read Chapter 14 for more information
on witnesses.

C. Police Accident Reports

It is always wise to have a police accident report prepared after any accident. They are admissible as evidence in Small Claims Court. The theory is that a cop investigating the circumstances of the accident at the scene is in a better position to establish the truth of what happened than is any other third party. So, if there is an accident report, buy a copy for a few dollars from the police station. If it supports you, bring it to court. If it doesn't, be prepared to refute what it says. This can best be done with the testimony of an eye witness. If both an eye witness and a police report are against you, try prayer.

D. Diagrams

After witnesses and police accident reports, the most effective evidence is a good diagram. It is almost impossible for a judge to understand how an accident happened using words alone. Several times I have seen a good case lost because the judge never

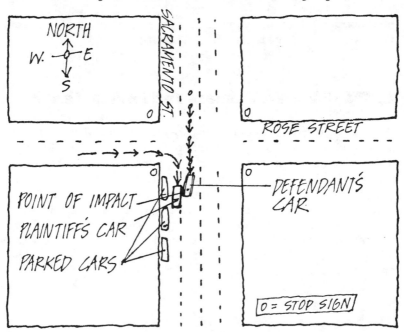

properly visualized what happened. All courtrooms
have blackboards, and it is proper to draw out what
happened as part of your presentation. If you are
nervous about your ability to do this, you may want
to prepare your diagram in advance and bring it to
court. Use crayons or magic markers and draw on a
large piece of paper about three feet square. Do a
good job with attention to detail. Here is a sample
drawing that you might prepare to aid your testimony
if you were eastbound on Rose St. and making a right
hand turn on Sacramento St. when you were hit by a
car that ran a stop sign on Sacramento. Of course,
the diagram doesn't tell the whole story--you have to
do that.

E. Photos

Photographs can sometimes be of aid in fender
bender cases. They can serve to back up your story
about how an accident occurred. For example, if you
claimed that you were sideswiped while you were

parked, a photo showing a long series of scratches down the side of your car would be helpful. It is also a good idea to have pictures of the defendant's car if you can manage to get them and photos of the scene of the accident.

F. Estimates

In a vehicle accident case you are entitled to recover for damage to your vehicle, personal injuries, uncompensated time off from work as a result of personal injuries, damages to things inside your car, and money for transportation while your car was out-of-commission.[2] Of course, major accidents will not be heard in Small Claims Court, and most Small Claims cases involve only damage to a vehicle. Get three written estimates for the cost of repairing the vehicle. If you have already gotten the work done, bring your cancelled check or receipt from the repair shop. Be sure to get your estimates from reputable shops. If, for some reason, you get an estimate from someone you later think isn't competent, simply ignore it, and get another. You have no responsibility to get your car fixed by anyone suggested to you by the person who caused the damage. Common sense normally dictates that you don't. Unfortunately, you can't recover money from the other party to cover the time you put in to get estimates, take your car to the repair shop, or appear in court.

DEFENDANT'S NOTE: Sometimes plaintiffs dishonestly try to get already existing damage to their car fixed as part of getting the legitimate accident work done. If you think the repair bill is high, try developing your own evidence that this is so. If you have a picture of the plaintiff's car showing the damage, this can be a big help. Also, remember that the plaintiff is only entitled to get repairs made up to the total value of the car before the accident.

---

2 See Chapter 5 for a more thorough discussion of damages. As far as getting money for transportation while your car is out-of-commission, you can only recover for the minimum time it would take to get your car fixed. Thus, if you could arrange to get a fender put right in one day, you are only entitled to a rent-a-car for one day, even if the mechanic takes four.

If the car was worth only $500 and the repairs would
cost $750, the plaintiff is only entitled to $500
(see Chapter 5).

G. Your Demand Letter

Here again, as in almost every other type of
Small Claims Court case, you should write a letter to
your opponent with an eye to the judge reading it.
See the examples in Chapter 6. Here is another:

---

18 Channing Way
Fullerton, Calif.

August 27, 19___

R. Rigsby Rugg
27 Miramar Crescent
Anaheim, Calif.

Dear Mr. Rugg:

On August 15, 19___ I was eastbound on Rose Street in Fullerton, California at about 3:30 on a sunny afternoon. I stopped at the stop sign
at the corner of Rose and Sacramento and then proceeded to turn right
(south) on Sacramento. As I was making my turn, I saw your car coming
southbound on Sacramento. You were about 20 feet north of the corner
of Rose. Instead of stopping at the stop sign, you proceeded across the
intersection and struck my car on the front right fender. By the time
I realized that you were coming through the stop sign, there was nothing
I could do to get out of your way.

As you remember, after the accident the Fullerton police were called
and cited you for failure to stop at a stop sign. I have gotten a copy
of the police report from the police and it confirms the facts as I have
stated them here.

I have gotten three estimates for the work needed on my car. The
lowest is $412. I am proceeding to get this work done as I need my car
fixed as soon as possible.

I will appreciate receiving a check from you as soon as possible. If
you wish to talk about any aspect of this situation, please don't hesit-
ate to call me, evenings at 486-1482.

Sincerely,

Sandy McClatchy

In court Sandy would present her case like this:

Clerk: "Next case, McClatchy v. Rugg. Please
come forward."

Judge: "Please tell me what happened, Ms.
McClatchy."

Sandy McClatchy: "Good morning. This dispute involves an auto accident that occurred at Rose and Sacramento Streets on the afternoon of August 15, 19__. I was coming uphill on Rose (that's east) and stopped at the corner. There is a four-way stop sign at the corner. I turned right, or south, on Sacramento Street, and as I was doing so, Mr. Rugg ran the stop sign on Sacramento and crashed into my front fender. Your Honor, may I use the blackboard to make a quick diagram?"

Judge: "Please do, I was about to ask you if you would."

Sandy McClatchy: (makes drawing like the one in Section D, points out the movement of the cars in detail and answers several questions from the judge) "Your Honor, before I sit down, I would like to give you several items of evidence. First, I have a copy of the police accident report from the Fullerton police which states that Mr. Rugg got a citation for failing to stop at a stop sign. Second, I have some photos which show the damage to the front fender of my car. Third, I have my letter to Mr. Rugg, trying to settle this case and finally I have several estimates of the cost of repairing the damage to my car. As you can see from my cancelled check, I took the lowest one."

Judge: "Thank you, Ms. McClatchy. Now, Mr. Rugg, it's your turn."

R. Rigsby Rugg: "Your Honor, my case rests on one basic fact. Ms. McClatchy was negligent because she made a wide turn into Sacramento Street. Instead of going from the right hand lane of Rose to the right hand, or inside lane, on Sacramento Street, she turned into the center lane on Sacramento Street. (Mr. Rugg moves to the blackboard and points out what he says happened.) Now it might be true that I made a rolling stop at the corner. You know, I really stopped, but maybe not quite all the way--but I never would have hit anybody if she had kept to her own side of the road. Also, your Honor, I would like to say this--she darted out; she has one of those little foreign cars and instead of easing out slow like I do with my Lincoln, she jumped out like a rabbit being chased by a red fox."

Judge: "Do you have anything else to say, Ms. McClatchy?"

Sandy McClatchy: "I am not going to even try to argue about whether Mr. Rugg can be rolling and stopped at the same time. I think the policeman who cited him answered that question. I want to answer his point about my turning into the center lane on Sacramento St., instead of the inside lane. It is true that, after stopping, I had to make a slightly wider turn than usual. If you will look again at the diagram I drew, you will see that a car was parked almost to the corner of Sacramento and Rose on Sacramento. To get around this car, I had to drive a little farther into Sacramento before starting my turn than would have been necessary otherwise. I didn't turn into the center lane, but as I made the turn, my outside fender crossed into the center lane slightly. This is when Mr. Rugg hit me. I feel that since I had the right of way and I had to do what I did to make the turn, I wasn't negligent."

Judge: "Thank you both—you will get my decision in the mail."

(The judge decided in favor of Sandy McClatchy and awarded her $412 plus service of process and filing costs.)

NOTE: As I discussed in Chapter 5, you can win, or partially win, a case involving negligence even if you were not completely in the right. If the other person was more at fault than you were, you have a case. This concept of "comparative" negligence is a new one in California. It used to be that, if you were even a little at fault, you couldn't recover.

20.

Landlord – Tenant Cases

Small Claims Court can be used by a tenant to sue for money damages for such things as the failure of a landlord to return a cleaning or damage deposit, invasion of the tenant's privacy, or landlord's violation of his duty to provide habitable premises, and rent control violations, to name but a few. A landlord might use it to sue a tenant or former tenant for damage done to the rental property. In some situations it is also possible for a landlord to seek to evict a tenant. This is an exception to the general rule that only money judgments can be handed down by Small Claims Courts. It makes great sense to use Small Claims Court for money damage cases, and a lot less sense to use it for evictions. Evictions are usually handled better in Municipal Court. Why? Because, in Small Claims Court, the defendant has an automatic right to appeal the eviction judgment and to remain living in the rental unit while the appeal is pending even though no rent is paid (see Section C below). This rule badly needs changing. Indeed, a lot of rules need changing so that all landlord-tenant cases can automatically be heard in a special division of Small Claims Court. Landlord and tenant both should have quick access to an inexpensive dispute resolution forum where hassles can be settled quickly, cheaply and fairly.

A. Deposit Cases

The most common landlord-tenant disputes concern the failure of a landlord to return a tenant's cleaning and damage deposits after the tenant moves out. These days, deposits can add up to many hundreds of dollars and tenants understandably want them returned.

Getting deposits back can be easy or difficult depending upon both the facts of the situation and on how much homework a tenant has done in advance of filing suit. Many landlords are experienced with Small Claims proceedings and come to court prepared with a long list of damaged and dirty conditions that they claim that the tenant left behind. All too often, the landlord's presentation leaves the tenant sputtering with righteous indignation. Unfortunately evidence, not indignation, wins cases. Think about it—if the tenant testifies the apartment was clean, and the landlord that it was dirty, the judge (unless he or she is psychic) is stuck making a decision that is little more than a guess. Faced with this sort of situation, most judges will split the difference.

How should a tenant prepare a case involving failure to return deposits? Ideally, preparation should start when he or she moves in. Any damage or dirty conditions should be noted as part of the lease or rental agreement. The tenant should also take photographs of substandard conditions and have neighbors or friends look the place over. When the tenant moves out and cleans up, s/he should do much the same thing—take photos, have friends check the place over, keep receipts for cleaning materials and try to reach an understanding with the landlord.[1]

In California the burden of proof that conditions exist which justify the landlord keeping all, or part, of a deposit falls on the landlord. The law also states that if a deposit is not returned within

---

1 All of this is discussed in more detail in The California Tenants' Handbook, Moskovitz, Warner and Sherman (order information at back of this book). The Tenants' Handbook contains a tear-out room-by-room inventory sheet so that the landlord and tenant can imspect the place on moving in and moving out and jointly record the results.

two weeks from the time the tenant moves out and if the landlord acted in bad faith in retaining the deposits, the tenant may be entitled to $200 in "punitive" damages, over and above the actual amount of the deposits.[2] Whether or not the tenant actually gets punitive damages is a matter of judicial discretion, but it never hurts to bring your suit for an amount that includes them.

Now let's assume that you are a tenant and have not gotten $300 in cleaning and damage deposits returned even though you moved out of an apartment three weeks ago, having paid all your rent and having given proper notice. Start by writing the landlord a letter like this:

1700 Walnut Street
Costa Mesa, Calif.

October 15, 19___

Anderson Realty Co.
10 Rose St.
Costa Mesa, Calif.

Dear People:

    As you know, until September 30, 19___, I resided in apartment #4 at 1700 Walnut Street and regularly paid my rent to your office. When I moved out, I left the unit cleaner than when I moved in.

    As of today, I have received neither my $150 cleaning deposit nor my $150 damage deposit. Indeed I have never received any accounting from you for any of my money. Please be aware that I know my rights under California Civil Code 1950.5 and that, if I do not receive my money within the next week, I will regard the retention of these deposits as showing "bad faith" on your part and shall sue you, not only for the $300 in deposits, but also for the $200 punitive damages allowed by Section 1950.5 of the California Civil Code.

    May I hear from you soon.

                Sincerely,

                Farah Shields

If you get no satisfactory response, file your case. Sometimes it is hard to know who to sue as rent isn't always paid to the owner, but to a manager or other agent. In California multiple occupancy buildings must have ownership information posted on

---

2 California Civil Code 1950.5.

the premises, or have the name of the owner or his agent for suit, on the rental agreement. If you are in doubt as to who owns your unit, you are probably safe if you sue both the person to whom you pay your rent, and the person who signed the rental agreement, unless you have received notice that the building has been transferred to a new owner, in which case you would sue that person.

On court day a well-prepared tenant would show up in court with as many of the following pieces of evidence as possible:

*   Photos of the apartment on moving in which show any dirt of damage that already existed.

*   Photos of the apartment on moving out which show clean conditions.

*   Receipts for cleaning supplies used in the final clean-up.

*   A copy of your written lease or rental agreement, if any.

*   A copy of a demand letter to the landlord such as the one set out above.

* One, or preferably two, witnesses who were familiar with the property and saw it after you cleaned up and who will testify that it was immaculate. People who helped in the clean-up are always particularly effective witnesses. If you also have a witness who saw the place when you moved in and who will say that it wasn't so clean (or damage already existed), so much the better.

* A copy of an inventory of conditions when moving in and moving out, signed by the landlord and tenant, if one was prepared.

Proceedings in court should go something like this:

Clerk: "Shields v. Anderson Realty. Please step forward."

Judge: "Good morning. Please tell me your version of the facts, Ms. Shields."

Farah Shields: "I moved into the cottage at 1700 Walnut St. in Costa Mesa in the spring of 19__. I paid Mr. Anderson here my first and last months' rent which totaled $400. I also paid him $300 in deposits. The deposits were divided $150 for cleaning and $150 for damage. Here is a copy of the rental agreement (hands it to the clerk) which specifically states that these deposits are to be returned to me if the apartment is left clean and undamaged.

When I moved into 1700 Walnut, it was a mess. It's a nice little cottage, but the people who lived there before me were sloppy. The stove was filthy, as was the bathroom, the refrigerator, the floors and just about everything else. In addition, the walls hadn't been painted in years. But I needed a place and this was the best available, so I moved in despite the mess. I painted the whole place-- everything. Mr. Anderson's office gave me the paint, but I did all of the work. And I cleaned the place thoroughly too. It took me three days. I like to live in a clean house.

Here are so pictures of what the place looked
like when I moved in (hands photos to clerk who gives
them to the judge). Here is a second set of photos
which were taken after I moved out and cleaned up
(again hands pictures to clerk). Your Honor, I think
these pictures tell the story--the place was clean
when I moved out. I also have receipts (hands to
clerk) for cleaning supplies and a rug shampooer that
I used during the clean-up. They total $18.25. I
have also brought two people who saw the place the
day I left and can tell you what it looked like."

Judge: (looking at one of the witnesses) "Do
you have some personal knowledge of what this cottage
looked like?"

John DeBono: "Yes, I helped Farah move in and
move out. I simply don't understand what the landlord is fussing about. The place was a smelly mess
when she moved in, and it was spotless when Farah
moved out."

Judge: (addressing the second witness) "Do you
have something to add?"

Puna Polaski: "I never saw 1700 Walnut when
Farah moved in because I didn't know her then. But I
did help her pack and clean up when she moved out. I
can tell you that the windows were washed, the floor
waxed and the oven cleaned because I did it. And I
can tell you that the rest of the cottage was clean
too, because I saw it."

Judge: "Mr. Anderson, do you want to present
your case."

Adam Anderson: "Your Honor, I am not here to
argue about whether the place was clean or not.
Maybe it was cleaner when Miss Shields moved out than
when she moved in. The reason I withheld the deposits is that the walls were all painted odd, bright
colors and I have had to paint them all over. Here
are some color pictures of the walls taken just after
Miss Shields moved out. They show several pink,
light blue and purple rainbows, a dancing hedgehog,
six birds apparently laughing, a purple dog, and

181

several unicorns of various sizes. I ask you, your Honor, how was I going to rent that place with a purple bulldog painted on the living room wall, especially with an orange butterfly on his nose? It cost me more than $300 to have the place painted over white."

Judge: (looks at the pictures and gives up trying to keep a straight face, which is O.K. as everyone in the courtroom is laughing except Mr. Anderson) "Let me ask a few questions. Was it true that the place needed a new coat of paint when you moved in, Ms. Shields?"

Farah Shields: "Yes."

Judge: "Do you agree, Mr. Anderson?"

Adam Anderson: "Yes, that's why my office paid her paint bills although we never would have if we had known about that bulldog, not to mention the rainbows."

Judge: "How much did the paint cost?"

Adam Anderson: "$65."

Judge: "I normally send decisions by mail, but today I am going to explain what I have decided. First, the apartment needed repainting anyway, Mr. Anderson, so I am not going to give you any credit for paying to have the work done. However, Ms. Shields, even though the place looks quite--shall I say, cheerful--decorated with its assorted wildlife, Mr. Anderson does have a point in that you went a little beyond what is reasonable. Therefore, I feel that it's unfair to make Anderson Realty pay for paint twice. My judgment is this: The $65 for the paint that was given to Ms. Shields is subtracted from the $300 deposits. This means that Anderson Realty owes Farah Shields $235 plus $9.00 for costs."

NOTE: We have focused here on deposits cases from the tenant's point of view. This is because tenants are the ones who initiate this sort of case. Landlords, too, though, should gain by carefully reading the list of evidence that is helpful in court. Often the best witness for a landlord is the new tenant who has just moved in. This person is likely to feel that the place isn't as clean as did the person who moved out.

B. Money Damage Cases—Unpaid Rent

Landlords most commonly initiate Small Claims actions to sue for unpaid rent. Often the tenant has already moved out and doesn't bother to show up in court. If this happens, the landlord wins by default. Sometimes the tenant does show up, but presents no real defense and is only there to request the judge to allow him to make payments over time (see Chapter 23 B).

The landlord should bring the lease or rental agreement to court and simply state the time periods for which rent is due, but unpaid. Nothing else is required unless the tenant claims that he did pay the rent. Sometimes a landlord will sue for three times the amount of rent owed (triple damages) under a lease or rental agreement that states that he is entitled to them if the tenant fails to pay rent, but stays in the rental unit. Doing this will almost guarantee that the tenant will put up a fight. In my experience landlords are rarely awarded more than their actual out-of-pocket loss, and it makes little sense to request more.

There are several valid defenses to a suit based on a tenant's failure to pay rent. The principal one is where the tenant claims that rent was withheld because the condition of the premises was "uninhabitable."[3] This amounts to the tenant saying to the landlord: "I won't pay my rent until you make necessary repairs."[4] It is legal to do this in California under the decision in <u>Green v. Superior</u>

---

[3] Under California law it is also legal for a tenant to have repairs done himself under some circumstances and deduct the cost from one month's rent. See California Civil Code Section 1941-42. This "repair and deduct" remedy is also discussed in detail in <u>The California Tenants' Handbook</u>.

[4] Often a tenant who fails to pay rent is brought to court by the landlord as part of an eviction action. If the tenant can prove that rent was withheld for a valid reason, he or she can't be evicted for exercising this right in California.

Court, 10 Cal. 3d 616.[5] The important thing for a tenant to understand is that rent withholding is not legal where the landlord refuses to fix some minor defect. For rent to be legally withheld, the condition needing repair must be sufficiently serious as to make the home "uninhabitable." In addition, the landlord must have been given reasonable notice of the problem. Thus, a broken furnace that a landlord refused to fix would qualify as a condition making a home uninhabitable in the winter, but lack of heat in the summer would not.

If you are involved in a rent withholding case as a tenant, your job is to prove (pictures, witnesses, etc.) that the condition that caused you to withhold rent is indeed serious. Thus, you might call the building inspector or an electrician to testify that the wiring was in a dangerous state of decay. The landlord, of course, has to prove the opposite--that the rental unit is in fundamentally sound shape, even though there may be some minor problems. A landlord has the right to inspect his/her properties at reasonable hours of the day as long as he/she gives the tenant reasonable notice. In California, 24 hours' notice is presumed by the law to be reasonable in the absence of an emergency. The landlord cannot use his/her right to inspect to harass the tenant, but the law has set down no absolute guidelines as to what harassment is.

Note: In place of the present cumbersome procedure which makes it difficult for a tenant to sue to get needed repairs made in Small Claims Court, we need to reform our landlord-tenant law to provide for an effective procedure which tenants can institute when a landlord abdicates his responsibility to properly maintain rental property.

■ ■ ■ ■ ■ ■ △▼△ ■ ■ ■ ■ ■ ■

---

5 If you are outside of California, check with a tenants' rights project or consumer group before withholding rent. Not all states allow rent withholding even when conditions are awful. If you are in California, see The California Tenants' Handbook, Moskovitz, Warner and Sherman, which goes into rent withholding and retaliation eviction in detail.

C. Evictions

Without question, landlords should have a simple and cheap way to free themselves of tenants who don't pay their rent. If a landlord wants to be sure to get a tenant out without ridiculous delays, an "unlawful detainer" action must be filed in Municipal Court. Traditionally, this has required the expense of a lawyer. There is now a book, <u>The California Landlord's Law Book</u>, available from Nolo Press[6] in January 1984, which tells landlords how to fill out the Municipal Court papers themselves.

As I said above, it is legal to do some types of evictions in Small Claims Court. This includes the situation where a tenant of residential property has a written or oral, month-to-month (or week-to-week) rental agreement and is behind in the rent.[7] If a lease is involved giving the tenant a set term of occupancy longer than 30 days, or if the eviction is for some reason other than non-payment of rent, the eviction action cannot be brought in Small Claims Court.

---

6 See back of this book for order information.

7 Before the landlord files an unlawful detainer (eviction) action, he or she must first serve the defendant (tenant) with a three-day notice to pay rent or leave the premises. A carbon of this notice should be retained to show the Small Claims Court. Only after the three-day notice has run out can an "unlawful detainer" be filed. The three-day notice may be personally served on the tenant by the landlord himself or by anyone else. A proof of service should be filled out (see Chapter 11).

The form necessary to bring an "unlawful·
detainer" (eviction) action in Small Claims Court
looks like this. (The form for Municipal Court is
quite different.)

L / OUT ®   Ubrco Business Forms ®

SMALL CLAIMS COURT OF CALIFORNIA, COUNTY OF ALAMEDA

BERKELEY - ALBANY JUDICIAL DISTRICT
2000 Center St. Berkeley, 94704

SC. NO (Fill in #)

PLAINTIFF   DEFENDANT

* John Landlord   * Tillie Tenant
  33 Orange   160 11th St.
  Berkeley, CA.   Berkeley, CA.

CLAIM OF PLAINTIFF

FOR UNLAWFUL DETAINER
                    John Landlord
                    (Name of Declarant or Plaintiff)
declare that prior to __SERVICE OF 3 DAY NOTICE.__
defendant(s) were tenants of plaintiff(s) in the premises described as __160 11th St., Berkeley, CA.__
_____
_____, California, at a rental of $__200.00__
per __month__ . payable __on the 1st__ ;that on __December 25__ defendant(s) were ____
indebted to plaintiff(s) in the sum of $__$175.00__ ; as rent for said premises; that on __Dec. 21__
plaintiff(s) served the attached notice on defendant(s); that defendant(s) have not paid any part of the rent demanded and are still in possession of the premises without consent of plaintiff(s); that the rental value of said
premises is $__200.00__ per month. **THIS CLAIMANT UNDERSTANDS THAT THE JUDGMENT ON
HIS CLAIM WILL BE CONCLUSIVE WITHOUT RIGHT OF APPEAL.**
I declare under penalty of perjury that the foregoing is true and correct.
Executed on __Dec. 25__ (Date) " __Berkeley__ (Place) ____   ____
                                                          Plaintiff or Declarant
                                              (Signature of landlord)

ORDER
The people of the State of California, to the within named defendant:
You are hereby directed to appear and answer the within and foregoing claim at the above entitled Court in Department_____ ,
at _____ M. On _____ ,and to have with you, then and there all books, papers and witnesses needed by
you to establish your defense to said claim. And you are further notified that in case you do not so appear, judgment will be given
against you in accordance with said claim as it is stated in said declaration and in addition costs of the action including costs of
service of the order.

                                                                          , CLERK
DATED_____   BY_____
                                                          DEPUTY CLERK

Date _____ — Hearing reset for _____ .at _____ M .Dept _____
Date _____ — Hearing reset for _____ .at _____ M .Dept _____
Date _____ — Hearing reset for _____ .at _____ M .Dept _____

Date of Proceeding	Proceedings (applicable only when dated and/or checked in box)	FEES, COSTS, ETC.	
		AMOUNT	RECEIPT NO
	Claim of Plaintiff, fees paid, order issued		
	Order and copy of declaration Mailed to defendant(s) by certified mail [ ]		
	Delivered to Plaintiff for personal service [ ]		

DOCKET COPY

FORM NO. 170-129

Why, if some evictions can be brought in Small
Claims Court, isn't it wise to do so? Because what
seems simple can often become cumbersome and complicated. Remember, the defendant-tenant has an automatic right to appeal from a Small Claims judgment.

186

If he exercises this right in an eviction action, he
can stay living in the property while the case is
transferred to the Superior Court. A tenant who
knows the rules can often delay eviction three or
four months by simply appealing the Small Claims
eviction decision, even though he pays no rent and
has no chance of winning the case in Superior Court.

Of course, the worst doesn't always happen.
Many times a tenant who is served with Small Claims
eviction papers moves out without a fight. If this
occurs, you are ahead of the game and have saved time
over the Municipal Court procedure. It's a bit of a
gamble, although you may be able to shorten the odds
a little by giving some thought to the personality
and sophistication of your tenant. If you think he
or she is going to try to hold on to the apartment
like a tick to a tasty dog, you had better go to
Municipal Court.

When a landlord gets to court, he need only
prove that the rent was not paid and that a correct
three-day notice was properly served.[8] Bring a copy
of the three-day notice to court and a "proof of
service" form filled out by the person doing the
service. The fact that a tenant is suffering from
some hardship such as illness, poverty, birth of a
child, etc., is not a defense to failure to pay rent.
Possible tenant defenses are discussed briefly in
Section B of this chapter. These include rent withholding and a tenant repairing an item himself or
herself and deducting the cost from the rent. A
tenant cannot legally raise a defect for the first
time on the day of the court hearing. The landlord
must be given reasonable notice that a defect exists
before rent is withheld, or repairs are made.

---

8 Under California law when a tenant fails to pay rent, a landlord
must first serve him (her) with a three-day notice to either pay the
rent or leave the premises. The notice must be in the alternative--a
notice that simply tells the tenant to get out is not legal and can
be challenged later by the tenant in court. Only after a proper
three-day notice has run out can the landlord legally start his
eviction action.

21.

Small Business, Small Claims

More and more, people who own or manage small businesses are turning to Small Claims Court to settle business disputes that they have been unable to compromise. They have learned that Small Claims Court is a relatively fast and cost efficient way to resolve business differences. Recent law changes allowing unincorporated businesses to appear in court in some circumstances without the need for business owners to be present have contributed to this increase in business usage (see Chapter 7).[1]

This chapter didn't appear in the first few editions of this book because I naively assumed that Chapter 18--CASES IN WHICH MONEY IS OWED--provided sufficient information to solve the problems of business people. It's here now because I have had so many requests from friends who own their own small businesses asking for additional information. It

---

1 Of course, incorporated businesses have long been able to authorize people other than the officers or other principles to appear in court (see Chapter 4).

turned out, of course, that although many disputes between small business people involve a simple failure to pay money, a significant number are much more complicated. Commonly these more complex disputes involve people who have had a continuing business relationship and find themselves in the midst of a major misunderstanding that goes beyond the refusal to pay a bill. Often both parties to the lawsuit are in court because they feel badly used--perhaps even "ripped off" or "cheated" by the other.

I have been asked for advice on preparing Small Claims Court cases by a surprising variety of business people. Requests for help have come from a dentist furious at a dental equipment wholesaler, an industrial designer who hadn't been paid for drawing preliminary plans, a typesetter being sued by his former accountant in a dispute involving the value of the latter's services, a landscape architect who was trying to enforce a verbal contract to increase his fee after a client asked for changes in final plans, and an author who claimed that her publisher had taken too long to publish her book. Although these disputes seem quite different from one another at first impression, they all turned out to have one thing in common--in each situation the disputants had enjoyed friendly business relationships at some time in the past. And in each case, at least part of the reason that the plaintiff brought the dispute to court involved feelings of anger and hurt.

A. Organizing Your Case

Business people normally have two great advantages over ordinary mortals when it comes to preparing for court. First, as a matter of course, they maintain a record-keeping system which includes files, ledgers, and increasingly, floppy disks. Taken together, these resources normally contain considerable raw material helpful to successfully proving even a fairly complicated case. The second advantage is more subtle, but no less real. It involves the average small business person's organizational skill--that is, his or her ability to take a confused mess of facts and organize them into a coherent and convincing narrative. Small business people who don't quickly develop good organizational skills commonly aren't in business long enough to even consider going to court. But the fact that business people begin with a little head start isn't usually much of an advantage when it comes to dealing with another business person. This is because two head starts have a way of cancelling one another out, with the only beneficiary being the judge, who gets to officiate a shorter, more coherent dispute.

Here are several hints that may be of real value when thinking about how to present a business case. This material is meant to supplement, not replace, the information contained in the rest of the book, particularly Chapters 2, 6, 13, 14, and 15. If you haven't already done so, I think you will find it helpful to read these chapters before continuing.

1. Contracts

Most business cases involve one person claiming that the other has broken a contract (see Chapter 2). Ask yourself the exact nature of the contract which was involved in your case. That is, what were your obligations and benefits from the deal, what was the other person supposed to do, and what was he or she going to get out of the deal?

Remember that oral contracts that can be carried out in one year (even if they actually take longer) are legal and enforceable in California. But remember too that oral contracts raise real problems in proving the facts.

You should also remember that a written contract need not be a formal document written on parchment and notarized by the Dalai Lama. Any letter or writing can constitute a contract. For example, if Hubert writes to Josephine, "I would like to order 1,000 gopher traps at $14.00 per trap," and Josephine writes back saying, "Thank you for your order. The traps will be sent next week," there is a contract. Indeed, if Josephine didn't write back at all but

simply sent the traps in a reasonable period of time,
there would also be a contract.

You should also be aware that the business usage
and practices in a particular field are commonly
viewed as being part of a contract and can be intro-
duced as evidence in Small Claims Court to support
your case. Thus, if Hubert ordered rodent traps in
February and Josephine didn't send them until
September, Hubert could present evidence in court
that everyone in the rodent control business knows
that traps are only saleable in the summer when
rodents attack crops and that Josephine's failure to
deliver the traps in the correct season constituted a
breach of contract.

And keep in mind that contracts can be, and
often are, changed many times as negotiations go back
and forth and circumstances change. The important
agreement is the last one.

2. Presenting Your Evidence In Court

a.   In business disputes, the problem is often
having too much evidence, rather than too little. If
this occurs, your job is obviously to separate the
material that is essential to proving yur case from
that which is less important. One good way to do
this is to organize both your verbal presentation and
the back-up evidence around the central issue in
dispute rather than trying to fill in all the back-
ground in an effort to work up to the point. Or, to
say the same thing in a different way, you usually
want to start with the end of your case rather than
the beginning. For example, if Ted did interior
decorating work for Alice and she called off the deal
in the middle, Ted would start his testimony with the
fact that a contract had existed to do the work and
that Alice broke it. The fact that Ted and Alice had
had dealings over the last several years which cast
light on the present dispute, or that Ted had turned
down another job to work for Alice, or that Alice had
made a number of unreasonable demands on him, might
well constitute good supporting evidence, but should
be alluded to only to the extent that they support

the main point. All too often I have seen people
tell a great but lengthy story in court, only to put
the judge to sleep before the main point was reached.

   b. Many business people have employees, partners, or business associates who have intimate knowledge of the dispute. By all means, bring them to
court as witnesses. A live witness is almost always
worth more than a stack of documentary evidence.

   c. In some situations, having a witness testify
as to the normal business practices in a field can be
helpful. Thus, if in your business payment is always
made within thirty days after delivery of goods and
the person you are having a dispute with claimed that
a 120-period schedule was adequate, you would want to
present an "expert" witness who could testify as to
normal business practices.

B. The Drama Of The Distraught Designer

   Now let's review a case that I was recently
asked about. Don is a successful industrial designer
who heads his own small company. He has offices in a
converted factory building near a major university
and prides himself on doing highly innovative and
creative work. Normally he is confident and cheerful, but one day when he stopped by the Nolo office
to say hello, he looked more than a little out of
sorts.

   "What's up?" I asked.

   "Oh, a couple of late nights of high pressure
work," Don replied.

   "What's new about that?" I asked him.

   "Well, that's not really what's bugging me.
Actually, I wonder if you can give me a little
advice."

   "Sure, what's the problem?"

"Well, I did some design work for an outfit that wants to build a small candle factory and I'm out $1,700. They claim that we never had a contract, but that's simply not true. What really happened is that they gambled and authorized me to do some preliminary work before they got their financing assured. When interest rates went through the roof, the whole deal collapsed. I had already completed my work, but they got uptight and refused to pay."

"So what are you going to do?" I asked him.

"Well, I got Stephanie Carlin, a lawyer who has done some work for me, to write them a letter, but that didn't do any good, so I took Stephanie's advice and filed a Small Claims Court suit against them myself."

"For how much?"

"For the Small Claims maximum. I had to scale down the claim to fit it in, but it was better than paying Stephanie's $75 an hour."

"How can I help?" I asked.

"Believe it or not, I've never been to court and I'm afraid I will overlook something or do something stupid, like calling the judge 'your holiness' instead of 'your honor.' I'm not much on bowing and scraping and the whole court rigamarole has always annoyed me."

"Okay, let me show you how simple your job is. First, how did the candle people (let's call them Wickless) contact you to set up the deal?"

"They are friends of friends. They called and we talked on the phone a couple of times. There was a lot of back and forth about how much I would charge for the whole job and how much for parts of it. After a little ordinary confusion, we decided that I would start with the preliminary drawings and be paid thirteen hundred dollars. If the whole job came through and we felt good about one another, I would do the whole thing."

"Did you write up a contract?"

"No, that's just it. On big jobs I always do, but this one was tiny. They just stopped by the next day and we hashed out the whole thing in person."

"Did you make notes?"

"Sure. In fact, I made a few sketches and then they gave me specifications and sketches they had made."

"Do you still have those?"

"Yes, and also a couple of letters they sent later thanking me for my good ideas and making a few suggestions for changes. And of course, I have copies of the detailed drawings I made and sent them."

"Well, that's it then," I said.

"What do you mean, that's it? You mean that I don't have a case?"

"Just the contrary. I mean you have just told me that you can prove that a contract exists. The combination of the sketches they provided and the letters they wrote you pretty well prove that they asked you to do the work. There is a strong presumption in law that when a person is asked to do work, he or she is to be paid if the work is completed. Now, in this sort of situation, I suspect that Wickless will raise one of two defenses if they bother to contest your claim at all. The first is that you were doing your work on speculation--that is, that the deal was that you were to be paid for your preliminary work only if the financing went through, and/or second, that your work was substandard in some way, such as not being what was agreed on."

"But they wrote me that my design was of excellent quality."

"Great, then that takes care of that issue. How about the other one? Do you ever do preliminary work without expecting to be paid unless the deal goes through? And is that a common way to operate in your business?"

"Me? Never! I don't have to. I suppose some designers do, or at least prepare detailed proposals without pay, but I have more work than I can decently do and I make it clear to all potential clients that I charge for preliminary drawings. In this situation, as I said, we agreed on the price in advance."

"What about witnesses to that conversation?"

"Well, Jim, my partner, sat in on one of the early discussions. We hadn't agreed on the final price yet, but we weren't too far apart."

"Was it clear to Jim that you intended to charge and that Wickless knew you did?"

"Yes, absolutely."

"Great, bring Jim to court with you. Here is how I would proceed. Organize your statement as to what happened so that it takes you no longer than five minutes to present it to the judge. Bring your sketches, and most important, the sketch the Wickless people made, along with the letters they sent you, and show them to the judge. Then have your partner testify to being present when money was discussed. You should have no trouble. If you're nervous about being in court, go down and check it out a few days before. It's just down at Center Street and I'm sure that if you watch for half an hour, you will be raring to go!"

NOTE: This little scenario is a simplified version of a real case. Don was given a judgment for the entire amount he requested and Wickless paid it.

C. Old Friends Fall Out

Sadly, this is a typical story. Tom, a true artist when it comes to graphics, is a bit ingenuous when it comes to dollars and cents. Recognizing this, he never tried to prepare his tax returns, but for several years had turned all of his tax affairs over to Phillip, a local C.P.A. Price was discussed the first year, but after that Tom just paid Phillip's bill when the job was done. One spring, things went wrong. As usual, Tom's records weren't great, and he was late in getting them to Phillip. Phillip was busy and put Tom's tax return together without discussing it with him in detail. When Tom saw the return, he was shocked. He felt that he was being asked to pay way too much to Uncle Sam. He called Phillip and reminded him of a number of deductions that he felt had been overlooked. There was some discussion of whether Phillip should have known about these or not. At this time, Phillip complained about Tom's sloppy records and his delay in making them available, and Tom told Phillip that he thought that Phillip had done a hurried and sub-standard job. After some more grumpy talk back and forth, Phillip agreed to make the necessary corrections. In a week this was done and the return was again sent to Tom. While his tax liability was now less, Tom was still annoyed, feeling that not all of the oversights had been amended. Tom called Phillip again and this time they quickly got into a shouting match which ended with Phillip very reluctantly agreeing to look at the return a third time and Tom saying that he was taking his business to an accountant who could add. Tom did just that and after several modifications were made, resulting in a slightly lower tax liability, the return was filed. The second accountant stated that as he needed to check all of Phillip's work to satisfy himself that it was right, he ended up doing almost as much work as if he had started from scratch. He billed Tom for

$500, saying that this was $250 less than if he had not had the benefit of Phillip's work.

Phillip billed Tom $1,200. Tom was furious and refused to pay. Phillip then sent Tom a demand letter stating that most of the problems were created by Tom's bad records, that he had made a number of changes when requested to do so and had offered to make the final changes at no additional charge. Tom replied with "I'll see you in court." Which is exactly what happened as Phillip went ahead with his suit.

Okay, now it's up to you. Imagine for a moment that you are Phillip. How would you prepare your case? In the spirit of not asking you questions I am afraid to answer myself, here is how I would proceed.

Phillip's Case

1. Phillip's first job is to write a clear, concise demand letter (see Chapter 7);

2. In court, Phillip will want to prove that he did work that was worth $1,200. Bringing copies of Tom's tax returns as well as his own work sheets is the simplest way to accomplish this. The returns should not be presented to the judge page by page, but as a package. The purpose is to indicate that a lot of work has been done, not go into details;

3. Phillip should then testify as to his hourly rate and how many hours he worked. He should mention that more hours were required than would otherwise have been the case because Tom did not have the raw data well organized. To illustrate his point, Phillip should introduce the raw data Tom gave him into evidence (i.e., a shoebox full of messy receipts);

4. Phillip has now presented his basic case, which is simply that he was hired to do a job, he did it, and he wasn't paid. However, Phillip would be wise to go beyond this and anticipate at least some of Tom's defenses, which will almost surely involve

the poor quality of the work done, as well as a claim that Phillip is simply charging too much. Therefore, were I Phillip, I would close my testimony with a statement along these lines:

"Your honor, when I finished my work my client pointed out that several deductions had been over-looked. I believed then and believe now that this was because the data he provided me with was inade-quate, but I did rework the return and corrected several items that were left out. When my client told me that he felt even the revised draft needed work, I again told him that I would work with him to make any necessary changes. It was at this point that he refused to let me see the returns and hired another accountant. In my professional opinion, very little work remained to be done at this stage-- certainly nothing that couldn't be accomplished in an hour or two. Now, as to the amount charged, it took me twelve hours to reconstruct what went on in the typesetting business from the mess of incomplete and incoherent records I was given. At $40 per hour, this means that almost $500 of my bill involved work that had to be done prior to actually preparing the return. Taking into consideration the difficult circumstances, I believe I charged fairly for the work I did, and that I did my work well."

Tom's Case

Okay, so much for getting into the head of an indignant accountant. Now let's see how Tom, the upset typesetter, might defend his case.

1. Tom should begin by writing a letter of his own, rebutting Phillip's demand letter point by point (see Chapter 7). He should bring this letter to court and give it to the judge;

2. Next, Tom should testify that he refused to pay the bill because he felt that Phillip's work was so poorly done that he didn't trust Phillip to finish

the job. Tom should testify as to the details of
several of the points that Phillip overlooked. Thus,
if Tom provided Phillip with information concerning
his purchase of a new typesetting machine and Phillip
forgot to claim the investment tax credit, this would
be important evidence. But Tom should be careful to
make his points relatively brief and understandable.
He won't gain by a long and boring rehash of his
entire return;

3. Now, to really make his case, Tom should
present more detailed evidence that supports his
claim that Phillip did his work poorly. The tax
return as correctly prepared by the new accountant
would be of some help, but far more valuable would be
having the second accountant come to court to testify. Unfortunately, professionals are commonly
reluctant to testify against one another, so this may
be difficult to arrange. But Tom should at the very
least be able to get a letter from the new accountant
outlining the things that he found it necessary to do
to change the return as prepared by Phillip;

4. Tom should also present to the court his
cancelled checks paid Phillip for the last several
years' returns, assuming, of course, that Phillip's
previous bills were much less. For example, if Tom
had been billed $400 and $500 in the two previous
years, it would raise some questions as to Phillip's
bill of $1,200 for the current year.

5. Tom should also present the bill from the
second accountant to the court as well as his note
explaining that his $500 charge was $250 less than
his normal bill for the whole job.

NOTE: After (or perhaps during) Phillip's and
Tom's testimony, the judge is almost certain to ask a
number of questions. In addition, he or she will
probably give each an opportunity to rebut the
statements of the other. I don't have space to discuss how this might go in detail, but in rebuttal,
generally it's important to focus on the one or two

points that you think the judge has missed or is in danger of getting wrong. This is not a time to attempt to restate your entire case.

What Happened?

Phillip was given a judgment for $400. The judge didn't explain his reasoning, but apparently felt that there was some right on each side and split the difference with a little edge to Tom. This sort of decision where each side is given something is common in Small Claims Court and again illustrates the wisdom of the parties' working out their own compromise. Even if Tom and Phillip had arrived at a solution where one or the other gave up a little more than the judge ordered, there would have been a saving in time and aggravation that probably would have more than made up the difference.

22.

Miscellaneous Cases

By now you should have a clear idea as to how any Small Claims case can be sensibly presented. The facts of each situation will vary, but the general approach will not. Here I will discuss a few more common case types. If I haven't covered yours in detail, simply make your own outline of steps to be taken adopting the general approaches I have suggested.

A. Clothing (Alteration And Cleaning)

Several years ago, before I started regularly attending Small Claims Court, I stopped by one morning when I had a few free moments to kill before a criminal hearing. The case being argued involved an elderly German-American gentleman with a strong accent, suing an equally aged Armenian tailor, who was also seriously uncomfortable with the English

language. The dispute centered around whether a
suitcoat that the tailor had made for the plaintiff
should have had two or three buttons. After ten
minutes of almost incomprehensible testimony, I
understood little more than that the plaintiff had
never owned a suit with two buttons and the tailor
had never made one with three. The two men ended by
standing facing one another--each pulling a sleeve of
the suitcoat and each yelling as loud as he could in
his own language, apparently about how many buttons a
suit ought to have. Much to their credit, the judge
and bailiff just sat and smiled. What happened? I
don't know. I was still actively practicing law then
and had to bustle off to argue before another judge
that my client thought that two ounces of marijuana
he was carrying in a money belt was really oregano.
You can probably guess how that argument ended.

While I have never seen another clothing case
quite as colorful as that of the two-button suit, I
have been consistently surprised at how often I have
encountered people in Small Claims Court, clutching
an injured garment. We must indeed come to view our
clothing as an extension of ourselves, because so many
of us react with an indignation out of proportion to
our monetary loss when some favorite item is damaged.
I will never forget the morning I saw a particularly
sour-looking fellow with neither word nor smile for
anyone, including his obviously long-suffering wife,
draw himself up to full height and wax poetic for
five minutes about a four-year-old leather vest that
a clean had mutilated.

Winning a significant victory in a case
involving clothing is often difficult. Why?
Because, while the liability is often easy to establish (i.e., the seamstress cut off the collar instead
of the cuff), damages are difficult or impossible to
prove in any reasonable amount for the obvious reason
that used clothing has little actual market value,
even though it may have cost a lot to start with or
have enormous sentimental value to its owner.
(Clothing cases are also discussed in Chapters 2 A
and 4 C.) In theory, a court can only award a
plaintiff the fair market value of the damaged
clothing, not its replacement cost. But because this

rule of law commonly works a severe injustice in clothing cases (a $400 suit bought last week may only be worth $100 used this week), many judges tend to bend it a little in favor of the person who has suffered the loss.

They do this by allowing an amount pretty close to the original purchase price when the clothing involved was almost new, even though its fair market value for resale would be much less. Thus, the owner of a $200 dress that had been ruined by a seamstress after only one wearing might recover $150. Judges are not required to take this approach, but many do. With older clothing, I have also seen some judges take a flexible approach. They do this by making a rough estimate as to the percentage of use that remains in a garment and then awarding the plaintiff this percentage of the original purchase price. Thus, if a cleaner ruined a $300 suit that had been worn for about 50% of its useful life, the plaintiff might recover $150.

Here are some hints:

* Bring the damaged clothing to court. It's hard for a tailor to say much when confronted with a coat that is two sizes too big or has three sleeves.

* Be ready to prove the original purchase price with a cancelled check, newspaper ad, credit card statement, etc.

* Be sure that the person you are suing (tailor, cleaner, seamstress, etc.) caused the problem. As noted in the example of the suede coat in Chapter 2, some problems that develop during cleaning or alterations may be the responsibility of the manufacturer.

NOTE: Cleaners particularly are prone to offer "proof" from "independent testing laboratories" that damage caused during cleaning wasn't their fault. You will want to ask: How much the cleaner paid the testing lab for the report? How many times had the same cleaner used the same testing lab before? How did the cleaner know about the testing lab (does it solict business from the cleaners?), etc.

B. Dog Bite Cases

Re-read Chapter 2 where I use several dog bite cases as examples. To review: be ready to prove the extent of the injury, the location where it occurred,

time off from work without compensation, doctors' bills, etc. If the dog is mean-looking, a picture will be a great help. If the dog bite occurred off the dog owner's property, you have an excellent chance of recovery. If the attack occurred on a part of the owner's property where you had a clear right to be (the front walk or even the backyard if you were there by invitation), you also stand to win. However, if you were on a part of the dog owner's property where people would normally not go without invitation and you had no such invitation, the chances are you will lose.

In cases where one dog attacks another, there is normally no recovery unless the attacking dog entered the other's property, or the attacking dog was loose and the victim was on a leash. When two loose dogs get into a mix-up on neutral ground, there is not usually an award of damages to the loser.

C. Police Brutality—False Arrest Cases

Now and then actions against the police end up in Small Claims Court. Usually the plaintiff is an irate citizen who has tried and failed to get an attorney to represent him in a larger suit and, as a last resort, has filed for $1,500, the Small Claims limit.[1] Put simply, most of the people I have seen bringing this sort of case have been run out of court in a hurry. Why? Because the police and jailors have excellent legal advice and aren't afraid to lie to back each other up. The unwritten rule in any law enforcement agency is to protect your own derriere first, and to protect your buddies' derrieres right after that. Cops are not going to politely sit still and collect black marks on their service records without fighting back. Most law enforcement people have testified many times before and know how to handle themselves.

The reason that many plaintiffs must use Small Claims Court to sue law enforcement people pretty much tells the story. Lawyers won't normally invest their time and money in this sort of case because they find them almost impossible to win. Does this mean that I believe that people bringing false arrest, police brutality and similar type cases are wasting their time? Balancing the trouble involved, against the unlikely chance of success, I would have to say yes. That said, let me also say that I believe that lots of things that make little sense at a practical level are worthwhile at many others. I can't help but admire people who will fight for principle, even though they have a small chance of winning.

---

1 In most cases of this sort, you will want to sue the city, county or state government that employs the officer as well as the individual involved. In California, before you can sue a government entity, you must promptly file an administrative claim (see Chapter 8).

If you do sue a cop, jailor or anyone else with a badge, be sure that you have several witnesses who will back you up, and won't be intimidated into keeping their mouths shut. Never, never rely on one officer to testify against another. They simply won't do it. It may be cynical, but it is also realistic to assume that all cops will tell whatever lies necessary to protect themselves and each other. This isn't always true, but it happens often enough so that you may as well be prepared for the worst. You would also be wise to spend a few dollars and talk to a lawyer who specializes in criminal cases. For a $50 fee, you can probably pick up some valuable pointers as to how to convince the judge that you were treated in an illegal and unreasonable way. way。

D. Damage To Real Property (Land, Buildings, Etc.)

There is no typical case of this nature, as facts vary greatly. So instead of trying to set down general rules, let's look at a situation that happened recently to a friend of mine。 (Let's call her Babette.)

Babette owns a cinder-block building that houses two stores. One morning when she came to work, she noticed water pouring in through the back of her building. Because the building was set into a hill, it abutted about eight feet of her uphill neighbor's land. (Let's call her neighbor Boris.) After three days of investigation involving the use of green dye in Boris's plumbing system, it was discovered that the water came from an underground leak in Boris's sewer pipe. At this point, Babette had spent considerable effort and some money to pay helpers to get the water moppped up before it damaged anything in the stores。

Instead of fixing the leak promptly, Boris delayed for four days. All of this time, Babette and her helpers were mopping frantically. Finally, when Boris did get to work, he insisted on digging the pipe out himself, which took another four days. (A plumber with the right equipment could have done it in one.) In the middle of Boris's digging, when his yard looked as though it was being attacked by a herd of giant gophers, it rained. The water filled the holes and trenches instead of running off as it normally would have. Much of it ran through the ground into Babette's building.

When the flood was finally over, Babette figured out her costs as follows:

First three days (before the source of the water was discovered)	$148 (for help with mopping)
Next four days (while Boris refused to cooperate)	$288 (for help with mopping)
Final four days (including day it rained)	$262 (for help with mopping)
One secondhand water vacuum purchased during rain storm	$200
Her own time, valued at $7.00 per hour	$500

Assuming that Boris is unwilling to pay Babette's costs, for what amount should she sue and how much is she likely to recover? If you remember the lessons taught in Chapter 2, you will remember that before Babette can recover for her very real loss, she must show that Boris was negligent or caused her loss intentionally. Probably she can't do this for the first three days, when no one knew where the water was coming from. However, once the problem was discovered and Boris didn't take immediate steps to fix it, he was clearly negligent, and she can recover at least her out-or-pocket loss ($550 for labor and $200 for the water vacuum). Can Babette also recover for the value of her own time? The answer to this question is <u>maybe</u>. If she could show that she had to close her store or take time off from a job to stem the flood, she probably could recover. Were I she, I would sue for $1,250 ($550 for labor she paid for, $200 for the vacuum, and $500 for the value of her own labor) and count on getting most of it.

23.

Judgment and Appeal

A. The Judgment

The decision in your case will be mailed to the address on record with the clerk any time from a few days to a few weeks after your case is heard. The exception to this rule is when one side doesn't show up and the other wins by default. Default judgments are normally announced right in the courtroom.[1] The truth is that in the vast majority of contested cases the judge has already made up his/her mind at the time your case is heard and notes down his/her decision before you leave the courtroom. Traditionally, decisions have been sent by mail because the court didn't want to deal with angry, unhappy losers, especially those few who might get violent. More recently, however, a number of judges are explaining their decisions in court, on the theory that both

---

1 In Chapters 10, 12 and 15 we discuss default judgments and the fact that people who have had defaults entered against them can often get them set aside if (1) they had a decent excuse for not being present, and (2) they notify the court clerk immediately of their desire to have the judgment set aside.

parties are entitled to know why a particular decision was reached. One progressive judge put his
policy as follows: "The only time I don't announce
[in court] is when I have phoning or research to do or
if I feel that one party will be unnecessarily
embarrassed in front of the audience."

Often when a judgment is entered against a person, he or she feels that the judge would surely have
made a different decision if he or she hadn't gotten
mixed up, or overlooked some crucial fact, or had
properly understood an argument. On the basis of my
experience on the bench, I can tell you that in the
vast majority of Small Claims cases, there is little
likelihood that the judge would change his or her
decision even if you had a chance to argue the whole
case over. In any event, you normally don't.[2] You
have had your chance and the decision has gone
against you. Don't call the judge, or go see him, or
send him documents through the mail. You had your
chance in court, you don't get another chance in the
judge's office (see D, below, for appeal rights).

NOTE: Now that a judgment has been entered, we
need to expand our vocabulary slightly. The person
who wins the case (gets the judgment) now becomes
"the judgment creditor" and the loser is known as
"the judgment debtor."

B. Time Payments

We have mentioned the fact that in California a
judge may order that the loser be allowed to pay the
winner over a period of time, rather than all at
once. The judge won't normally make this sort of
order unless you request it. So, if you have no real
defense to a claim, or if you have a fairly good case
but aren't sure which way the judge will go, be sure
that the judge knows that, if the judgment goes
against you, you wish to have time to pay. You might
put your request this way:

---

2 There is one possible exception to this rule. If your case was
heard by a "pro tem" judge (see Chapter 13 G) and you feel it was
obviously decided wrong, it may be worth immediately sending a short
written statement to the presiding judge of the local Municipal
Court. Title it "Motion for Rehearing." This probably won't work,
but it's worth a try.

* "In closing my presentation, I would like to say that I believe I have a convincing case and should be awarded the judgment, but in the event that you rule for my opponent, I would like you to allow me time payments of no more than (whatever amount is convenient) per month."

Or, if you have no real defense:

  * "Your Honor, I request that you enter the judgment against me for no more than (an amount convenient to you) per month."

```
 1
 2
 3          SMALL CLAIMS COURT, FOR _____
 4       JUDICIAL DISTRICT, COUNTY OF _____, STATE OF CALIFORNIA
 5
 6   JOHN TOLLER,                )
 7              Plaintiff        )        Action Number SC._____
 8   v.                         )
 9   MILDRED EDWARDS,            )        PETITION, NOTICE OF MOTION,
                                 )        AND ORDER ALLOWING JUDGMENT TO BE
10              Defendant.       )        PAID IN INSTALLMENTS.
11
12       Comes now MILDRED EDWARDS and represents to the court that a judgment was
13   entered against her in the above entitled action in the amount of $526.00.  That
14   payment of this entire judgment immediately will cause a severe hardship to
15   MILDRED EDWARDS because ___(of lack of employment, or illness or whatever)___.
16   Petitioner can pay $25.00 per month.
17       Wherefore petitioner requests that an order by made to allow payment in
18   this amount.
19
20   DATED:_____        _____
21                                          PETITIONER
22                   NOTICE OF MOTION
23       To JOHN TOLLER.  Please take note that you are ordered to appear in court
24   on ___(date)_____ at ___(time)_____ to give any legal reason why
25   it shall not be ordered that the judgment in the above entitled case be paid in
26   installments of $25.00 per month.
27
28   DATED:_____   _____
                                            JUDGE
```

If you neglect to ask for time payments in court and wish to make this request after you receive the judgment, first contact the other party to see if he will voluntarily agree to accept his money on a schedule you can afford to pay. If he or she agrees, it would be wise to write your agreement down and each sign it. If your opponent is an all-or-nothing

1	ORDER
2	Judgment to be paid $25.00 on the first day of each month until fully
3	paid. Should the judgment debtor fail to make one or more payments the judgment
4	creditor may file an affidavit so stating with this court and the above order
5	shall thereby be vacated and the clerk shall proceed as if it had not been made.
6	
7	DATED: _____ _____
8	JUDGE
9	
10	

sort of person and refuses payments, promptly contact the court clerk and ask that the case again be brought before the judge--not as to the facts, but only to set up a payment schedule that you can live with.

C. Satisfaction Of Judgment

Here is a sample "Satisfaction of Judgment" form which is available from the Small Claims Court clerk. It must be signed by the judgment creditor. It is a good idea to get the satisfaction form filled out and signed when you pay the judgment. This saves the trouble of having to track down the other party later. Besides, people are much more willing to be cooperative when you are waving money under their noses than when they have already spent it. Once signed, you file the Satisfaction of Judgment with the Small Claims Court clerk. This clerk can give you a certified copy of the satisfaction if you ever need one.

ATTORNEY OR PARTY WITHOUT ATTORNEY *(Name and Address)*:

TELEPHONE NO.

FOR RECORDER'S OR SECRETARY OF STATE'S USE ONLY

ATTORNEY FOR *(Name)*:

NAME OF COURT:

STREET ADDRESS:

MAILING ADDRESS:

CITY AND ZIP CODE:

BRANCH NAME:

PLAINTIFF:

DEFENDANT:

CASE NUMBER

ACKNOWLEGMENT OF SATISFACTION OF JUDGMENT

☐ FULL ☐ PARTIAL ☐ MATURED INSTALLMENT

FOR COURT USE ONLY

1. Satisfaction of the judgment is acknowledged as follows *(see footnote* before completing)*:
   a. ☐ Full satisfaction
      (1) ☐ Judgment is satisfied in full.
      (2) ☐ The judgment creditor has accepted payment or performance other than that specified in the judgment in full satisfaction of the judgment.
   b. ☐ Partial satisfaction
      The amount received in partial satisfaction of the judgment is
      $
   c. ☐ Matured installment
      All matured installments under the installment judgment have been satisfied as of *(date)*:
2. Full name and address of judgment creditor:

3. Full name and address of assignee of record, if any:

4. Full name and address of judgment debtor being fully or partially released:

5. a. Judgment entered on *(date)*:
      ☐ (1) in judgment book volume no.:   (2) page no.:
   b. ☐ Renewal entered on *(date)*:
      ☐ (1) in judgment book volume no.:   (2) page no.:

6. ☐ An ☐ abstract of judgment ☐ certified copy of the judgment has been recorded as follows *(complete all information for each county where recorded)*:

COUNTY	DATE OF RECORDING	BOOK NUMBER	PAGE NUMBER

7. ☐ A notice of judgment lien has been filed in the office of the Secretary of State as file number *(specify)*:

NOTICE TO JUDGMENT DEBTOR: If this is an acknowledgment of full satisfaction of judgment, it will have to be recorded in each county shown in item 6 above, if any, in order to release the judgment lien, and will have to be filed in the office of the Secretary of State to terminate any judgment lien on personal property.

Date:

▶

(SIGNATURE OF JUDGMENT CREDITOR OR ASSIGNEE OF CREDITOR OR ATTORNEY)

*The names of the judgment creditor and judgment debtor must be stated as shown in any Abstract of Judgment which was recorded and is being released by this satisfaction. A separate notary acknowledgment must be attached for each signature.

Form Approved by the
Judicial Council of California
EJ-100 [Rev. July 1, 1983]

ACKNOWLEDGMENT OF SATISFACTION OF JUDGMENT

CCP 724.060, 724.120
724.250

1. The Right To A "Satisfaction Of Judgment"

The law states that a "judgment creditor" must file a "satisfaction of judgment" form with the court when he or she is paid (Code of Civil Procedure Section 117.9). If a judgment creditor who receives payment in full on a judgment fails to do this, the judgment debtor should send a written demand that this be done. A first class letter is adequate. If, after written demand, the judgment creditor still doesn't file his satisfaction without just cause, the judgment debtor is entitled to recover all actual damages he or she may sustain by reason of such failure and, in addition, shall be awarded $50 by way of punitive damages.

2. Getting A "Satisfaction Of Judgment" From A Person You Can't Find

Sometimes people forget to get a "Satisfaction of Judgment" when they pay a judgment, only to find later that they can't locate the judgment creditor. If this happens, consult the court clerk. You will have to prepare an affidavit as to your unsuccessful attempt to find the judgment creditor and submit it to the court with your proof that the judgment was paid.

D. The Appeal

If, in the face of justice, common sense and all of your fine arguments, the judge turns out to be a big dummy and rules for your opponent, you can appeal to a higher court, right? Not necessarily. In Small Claims Court if you are the person who brought the suit (the plaintiff) and you lose, you are finished, done, through. Plaintiffs have absolutely no right to appeal anywhere. Why? Because that's how the legislature made the rules. However, if you are the defendant and lose, you can appeal to the Superior Court if, and only if, you do it promptly.

Isn't it unfair, maybe even unconstitutional, to allow appeal rights for defendants and none for plaintiffs? I will leave it to you to decide the fairness issue, but it's not unconstitutional for the simple reason that a plaintiff knows before he files that he doesn't have a right to an appeal. He has a choice of bringing his suit in Small Claims Court where there is no right for plaintiffs to appeal, or in Municipal Court where both sides can appeal. The defendant doesn't have this opportunity to pick the court and, therefore, the legislature decided that his or her appeal rights should be preserved.

214

E. Filing Your Appeal

Now let's look at the mechanics of the appeal. In California, the defendant must file a notice of appeal within 20 days of the entry of the judgment. As judgments are mailed, this means that there will be less than 20 days to file an appeal from the day that the defendant receives the judgment. The date the judgment was entered will appear on the judgment. If for some reason attributable to the magic of the U.S. Postal Service your judgment doesn't show up within 20 days after it was entered, call the Small Claims clerk immediately and request help in getting an extension of time to file your appeal.

To file your notice of appeal, go to the Small Claims clerk's office and fill out a paper such as the one illustrated below. Currently, the appeal fee is close to $25. You are now going into Superior Court and you must pay according to their fee schedule. There is no charge for the original plaintiff to appear in Superior Court on an appeal. Indeed, if the Small Claims judgment is affirmed in whole or in part or the appeal is dismissed, the defendant shall not only be ordered to pay the amount of the judgment, but also interest, costs and the sum of $15 as an attorney fee.

When you file your appeal, the court will notify the other side that you have done so. You need not do this yourself. Once your appeal is on file at the Superior Court, your next step is to wait. When you are done waiting, you will probably have to wait some more. You are in the formal court system now, where traditionally very little happens, very slowly. Those who have been in the armed services will understand. All the deadlines apply to you--never to the bureaucracy. Eventually (two to six months depending on the county) you will get a notice giving you a court date in the Superior Court.[3]

---

3   Remember, in Chapter 20 I said that landlords can get into real trouble if a defendant appeals an eviction order. This is because the tenant can stay in the unit while the appeal is pending. This rule needs to be changed, or appeals must be greatly speeded up.

You are entitled to have an attorney in Superior
Court. But as your case is not worth a lot, you will
probably decide that it is not wise to hire one.
Indeed, there should be little practical reason for
an attorney, as you probably have an excellent grasp
of the issues by this time. Appeals are conducted
under the same informal rules that apply to regular
Small Claims Court hearings.

An appeal of a Small Claims judgment is not the
sort of appeal that the U. S. Supreme Court hears.
The Supreme Court, and the other formal appellate
courts, are concerned with looking at the written

record of what went on in a lower court with the idea
of changing a decision when a judge has misinter-
preted the law. Since no record has been made in
Small Claims Court, the Superior Court has nothing to
look over. They must start from scratch, as if
nothing had been said in Small Claims Court. You
simply argue the case over, presenting all your witnesses, documents, etc. Of course, both sides should
give some thought to how their presentation can be
improved. This is particularly true of the defendant, who has already lost once.

But what if your opponent hires an attorney on
appeal? Aren't you at a disadvantage if you represent yourself? Not really, because the appeal court
must follow the same informal rules (Judicial Council
Rule 55) as used in Small Claims Court. This means
the formal rules of evidence and procedure normally
used in Superior Court can't be followed on your
appeal. This should put you on a fairly equal
footing with the lawyer. If you have prepared carefully, you may even have an advantage; you carry with
you the honest conviction that you are right while a
lawyer arguing a Small Claims appeal always seems a
bit pathetic. If, despite common sense, you still
feel a little intimidated, however, the best cure is
to go watch a few Small Claims appeals. Ask the
Superior Court clerk when they are scheduled.

JURY TRIAL NOTE: In theory, either side may ask
for a jury trial on appeal. This is generally stupid
as jury fees must be posted in advance. In the
unlikely event you do face such a trial, simply present your case as you would to a judge.[4]

DISCOVERY NOTE: As this book goes to press,
there is a furious legal argument as to whether formal pretrial methods such as depositions, written
interrogatories, etc. can be used in Small Claims
appeals. These can slow appeals at the same time
they favor lawyers who know all the tricks. We look
forward to the day when they are clearly eliminated.

---

4 Smith v. Superior Court, 93 CA 3d 977.

24.

Collecting Your Money

O.K., you won, what does that mean? Simply that
you are entitled to the dollar amount of the judgment
from the opposing party or parties. How are you
going to get it? Try asking politely. This works in
the majority of cases, especially if you have sued a
respectable business. If you don't have personal
contact with the person who owes you the money, try a
note. Plaintiffs should wait 20 days after the day
the judgment is entered before trying to collect.1
If you make your request for money too soon, you may
remind the defendant to take advantage of his right
to appeal.

If you receive no response to your polite note,
you will have to get serious about collecting your
money or forget it. The emphasis in the previous
sentence is on the word "you." Much to many people's
surprise, the court does not enforce its judgments
and collect money for you--you have to do it yourself.

---

1 Unless they have gotten their judgment on the basis of the defendant's default. In this situation you may want to begin collection
activities immediately as the defendant has no right to appeal unless
the default judgment is vacated (see Chapter 10).

```
                    SAMPLE COLLECTION NOTE

                              P.O. Box 66
                              Berkeley, Calif.

                              February 15, 19___

     Mildred Edwards
     11 Milvia Street
     Berkeley, Calif. 94706

     Dear Mrs. Edwards:

         As you know, a judgment was entered against you in Small Claims Court
     on January 15 in the amount of $457.86.  As the judgment creditor I will
     appreciate your paying this amount at your earliest convenience.

         Thank you for your consideration.
                                        Very truly yours,


                                        John Toller
```

There are only a few relatively easy ways to collect money from a debtor. We mentioned these briefly in Chapter 3. Hopefully you gave some thought to collection before you brought your case. If you only now realize that your opponent doesn't have the money to buy a toothbrush and never will, you are better off not wasting more time and money trying to get him to pay up. Also, remember that a judgment is valid for ten years and can be renewed for an additional ten if you can show that you have tried to collect it, but failed. In some situations you may simply want to sit on it, with the hope that your "judgment debtor" will show a few signs of life in the future.

A. Levying On Wages, Bank Accounts, Business Assets, Real Property, Etc.

If a polite letter doesn't work (two weeks is plenty of time to wait), and you know that the person who owes you the money (the "judgment debtor") has it, you will have to start acting like a collection agency.[2]

If you know where the judgment debtor works, you are in good shape. Federal and state law allow you to get approximately 25% of a person's net wages to satisfy a debt.[3] Knowing where a judgment debtor banks can also be extremely valuable as you can order a sheriff or marshal to levy on a bank account and get whatever it contains at the time of the levy.[4] Of course, a bank account levy will only work once as the debtor is pretty sure to move his account when he realizes that you have emptied it. Other types of property are normally much more difficult to grab. Why? Because California has a number of "exemption" laws which say that, even though a person owes money, certain types of his/her property can't be taken to satisfy the debt. Items protected include a family house with $45,000 in equity, furniture, clothes, and much more. Practically speaking, the only assets other than wages and bank accounts that are normally worth thinking about to satisfy a Small Claims judgment are motor vehicles in which the judgment debtor has an equity of more than $1,200, real property other than the place where the debtor lives, and the receipts of an operating business. Theoretically, there are many other assets that you could reach, but in most cases they are not worth the time and expense involved, considering that your judgment is for the Small Claims maximum, or less.[5]

---

2 It is possible to turn your debt over to a real collection agency, but this probably doesn't make too much sense as the agency will take 50% of what they can collect. Unless you are a regular customer, the agency probably won't treat your debt with much priority unless they believe that it is easy to collect. If it is easy for them to collect, it probably won't be hard for you to do it yourself and save the fee.

3 If a person has a very low income, the amount your can recover can be considerably less than 25%.

4 Bank account levies are subject to the exempt property laws. Approximately 75% of wages in a bank account are exempt (100% if there has been a previous wage attachment involving the same money) for 30 days after payment. Social security money in a bank account is exempt.

5 You will find a complete list of exempt property and a thorough discussion of debtors' rights including bankruptcy in The California Debtors' Handbook--Billpayers' Rights, Warner and Honigsberg, Nolo Press.

1. The Writ Of Execution

Before you can levy on a person's wages or other property, you need to get a court order called a "Writ of Execution." If you have a Small Claims judgment, you are entitled to this writ. You get your Writ from the Small Claims Court clerk who will help you fill it out. The charge is $3.00, which is a recoverable cost (see C next page).

```
ATTORNEY OR PARTY WITHOUT ATTORNEY (Name and Address):        TELEPHONE NO:        FOR RECORDER'S USE ONLY
☐  Recording requested by and return to:

    John Toller                          (415) 845-0000
    P.O. Box 66
    Berkeley, CA 94702
ATTORNEY FOR ☐ JUDGMENT CREDITOR   ☐ ASSIGNEE OF RECORD
NAME OF COURT: (fill in court)
STREET ADDRESS:
MAILING ADDRESS:
CITY AND ZIP CODE:
BRANCH NAME:

PLAINTIFF:  John Toller
DEFENDANT:  Mildred Edwards                                  CASE NUMBER:

  WRIT OF  ☐ EXECUTION (MONEY JUDGMENT)
           ☐ POSSESSION OF ☐ Personal Property              FOR COURT USE ONLY
                          ☐ Real Property
           ☐ SALE

1. To the Sheriff or any Marshal or Constable of the County of: (fill in county
     where the assets are located)
   You are directed to enforce the judgment described below with daily interest and
   your costs as provided by law.
2. To any registered process server: You are authorized to serve this writ only in accord
   with CCP 699.080 or 715.040.
3. ☐ Judgment creditor ☐ Assignee of record
   (name): John Toller
4. Judgment debtor (name and last known address):

     Mildred Edwards
                                              9. ☐ Real or personal property to be delivered under a writ of posses-
                                                    sion or sold under a writ of sale is described on reverse.
                                             10. ☐ This writ is issued on a sister-state judgment
                                             11. Total judgment . . . . . . . . . . . $
                                             12. Costs after judgment (per filed
                                                 order or memo CCP 685.090) . $
         ☐ additional judgment debtors on reverse   13. Subtotal (add 11 and 12) . . . . . $ _____
5. Judgment entered on (date): (clerk will supply  14. Credits . . . . . . . . . . . . . . . . . $
6. ☐ Judgment renewed on (dates): this             15. Subtotal (subtract 14 from 13) . $ _____
                              information)          16. Interest after judgment (per filed
7. Notice of sale under this writ                       affidavit CCP 685.050) . . . . . . $
   a. ☐ has not been requested.                    17. Fee for issuance of writ . . . . . $
   b. ☐ has been requested (see reverse).          18. Total (add 15, 16, and 17) . . . . $ _____
8. ☐ Joint debtor information on reverse.          19. Levying officer: Add daily interest
   [SEAL]                                               from date of writ (at the legal rate
                                                        on 15) of . . . . . . . . . . . . . . . $

                                             20. ☐ The amounts called for in items 11–19 are different for each debtor.
                                                    These amounts are stated for each debtor on Attachment 20.

              Issued on
              (date):               Clerk, by _____ , Deputy
         ─ NOTICE TO PERSON SERVED:  SEE REVERSE FOR IMPORTANT INFORMATION
                        (Continued on reverse)
Form Approved by the
Judicial Council of California        WRIT OF EXECUTION
EJ-130 (Rev. July 1, 1983)                                          CCP 699.520
```

(fill in the correct amounts)

2. The Sheriff (Or Marshal)

Once your "Writ of Execution" form is filled out, take or send it to the sheriff or marshall in the county where the assets are located. The Small Claims Court clerk will do this for you if you request that they do so. Do it right away, as the Writ of Execution expires in 60 days if it is not served by the sheriff or marshall. If this time runs out, you will have to go back to the Small Claims clerk and get another "Writ of Execution" issued. Give the sheriff (marshal) or Small Claims clerk:

a. The "Writ of Execution" (original) and one to three or more copies depending on the asset to be collected;[6]

b. His fees for collecting (this will vary as to the type of asset, so you should inquire);

c. Instructions on what and where to collect. The sheriff, marshal or Small Claims clerk may have a form they wish you to use when giving them instructions. Ask about the fee when you call. Normally a letter is sufficient.

3. How To Levy On Wages And Bank Accounts

To seize a person's wages or bank account, you need the original and one copy of a "Writ of Execution," $14.00 for the sheriff (marshal) fee, and a letter of instruction:[7]

---

6 Don't forget to keep a copy of the "Writ of Execution" for your files.

7 The sheriff's or marshal's fee is different in some counties. Call the marshal's office or the "civil division" of the sheriff's office to find out the exact amount.

```
                              P.O. Box 66
                              Berkeley, Calif.

                              March 1, 19___

Sheriff (Civil Division), Alameda County
Alameda County Courthouse
Oakland, California
                         Re: John Toller v. Mildred Edwards
                             Albany-Berkeley Judicial Dist-
                             rict
                             Small Claims Court No. 81-52
Dear Sir:

    Enclosed you will find the original and one copy of a Writ of Execu-
tion issued by the Small Claims Court for the Oakland Judicial District
in the amount of $___(fill in total due)___.  I also enclose a check
for your fee in the amount of $_____.

    I hereby instruct you to levy on the wages of Mildred Edwards, who
works at the Graphite Oil Co., 1341 Chester St., Oakland, Calif.  Please
serve the Writ on or before March 15, 19___. 8


                              Very truly yours,



                              John Toller
```

4. Levying On Motor Vehicles (Including Planes, Boats and R.V.'s)

Getting money from wages or bank accounts is
fairly easy. Selling a person's motor vehicle is
more difficult for several reasons, including the
following:

a. $1,200 aggregate equity in one or more motor
vehicles is exempt from your levy (California Code of
Civil Procedure 704.010).

EXAMPLE: A judgment debtor has two cars worth
$4,000 on which he owes $3,000. This means that his
equity is $1,000--the bank owns the rest. As an
equity of $1,200 is exempt under C.C.P. 704.010, you

---

8 For a bank account, you would simply substitute "all monies in the
checking account of Mildred Edwards, located at the Bank of Trade, 11
City St., Oakland, CA." Where a bank account is in the name of the
defendant and someone else, you will have to post a bond for twice
the amount in the account to levy. Ask the sheriff or marshal for
details.

would end up with nothing.

b. One motor vehicle is exempt from attachment up to $2,500 if it is a "tool of a person's trade" (California Code of Civil Procedure 704.060).

EXAMPLE: A "judgment debtor" has a pickup truck worth $2,000 which she uses every day in her gardening business. The truck would be exempt.

c. The judgment debtor may not own the car he drives. It may be in someone else's name, or he may owe a bank or finance company as much or more than the car is worth.

To find out if a judgment debtor owns the car he drives, go to the Department of Motor Vehicles and give them the license number. For a small fee, they will tell you who owns the car, including whether or not a bank or finance company is involved. Once you have this information, you can determine whether it is worthwhile to have the sheriff pick up the car and sell it. Levying on motor vehicles can be expensive. The storage fees and the sheriff's cost of sale average over $200 and must be paid in advance. This money is recoverable when the vehicle is sold. Call the sheriff or marshall (Civil Division) of the county in which the car is located to find out how much money he requires as a deposit with your Writ of Execution and how many copies of the Writ you need. Then write the following letter:

P.O. Box 66
Berkeley, Calif.

March 1, 19___

Sheriff (Civil Division)
Alameda County
Alameda County Courthouse
Oakland, California

Re: John Toller v. Mildred Edwards
Small Claims Court
Albany-Berkeley Judicial District
No. SC 81-52

Dear Sir:

You are hereby instructed, under the authority of the enclosed Writ of Execution, to levy upon and sell all of the right, title and interest of Mildred Edwards, judgment debtor, in the following motor vehicle:

```
(Type here all information regarding the description of the
    car from your D.M.V. report, including the license number.)

    The vehicle is registered in the name(s) of Mildred Edwards and is
    regularly found at the following address(es):

    (List home and work address of owner)

    Enclosed is my check for $_____ to cover your costs of levy and
    sale.



                                    Very truly yours,



                                    John Toller
```

5. Real Property

It normally makes little sense to go through the complicated procedures involved in selling, or trying to sell, a person's real property to satisfy a Small Claims judgment--especially when the simple act of recording an "Abstract of Judgment" at the County Recorder's office in any (or all) counties where the judgment debtor owns real property gives you a lien against all of his real property in that county. When the judgment debtor wishes to sell his real property, the title will be clouded by your lien and he will have to pay you off to be able to transfer clear title to a third party. Thus, sooner or later, you will get your money.[9]

To record your judgment against real property, first get an "Abstract of Judgment" from the Small Claims clerk's office. The clerk will prepare this paper for you. Then take the "Abstract of Judgment" to the County Recorder's office in the county where the property is located, pay a fee and give the Recorder the mailing address of the judgment debtor so that they can be notified. They will do the rest.

---

[9] The only exception to this rule is that a home on which the judgment debtor has filed a homestead prior to your filing your "Abstract of Judgment" can be sold and the money (up to $45,000 in equity for a family, the blind or single persons over 65, and $30,000 for a single person under 65) used to buy another homesteaded home within six months without paying off your lien. If you wish information as to how to fill out the simple form necessary to homestead your house, see Protect Your Home With A Declaration of Homestead, Warner, Sherman and Ihara, Nolo Press.

6. Other Personal Property

Normally, it isn't worth the trouble to try to
levy on small items of personal property such as
furniture or appliances because they are commonly
covered by one or another of the state exemption laws
which state that certain possessions are exempt from
being taken to satisfy debts. The exemption laws are
found listed in C.C.P. Section 704.010 et seq. and
include furniture, clothing, some equity in motor
vehicles and much more.

7. Business Assets

It is possible to have someone from the sheriff's or marshal's office sent to the business of a
person who owes you money to collect it from the cash
on hand. This can be done in three ways as follows:

a. Till Tap: A deputy goes to the business one
time and picks up all the money in the till. The fee
for this is $14 plus a deposit.

    b. Eight Hour Keeper: A deputy stays all day at the place of business and collects all the money that comes in. Average fee--$35-$70. There is a deposit requirement.

    c. 48 Hour Keeper: The deputy stays at the business for a much longer period of time and collects what comes in. Average fee--$200-$350 depending on the county.

    Talk to the sheriff or marshal in your area to get more details. They will want an original and three copies of your Writ of Execution as well as instructions telling them where and when to go.

8. Pensions And Retirement Benefits

    You can get at money in individual or self-employment retirement plans held in any bank or savings institution. You go after this money just as you do any other money kept in a bank. Of course, you need to know where the money is.

Private company retirement plans and state or local government retirement plans can't be touched until the money is paid over to the employee.

Federal government payroll checks and pension and retirement benefits may not be garnisheed to satisfy any debts, except those for alimony and child support.

B. Finding Phantom Assets—The Judgment Debtor's Statement

As you now understand from reading the above section, collecting money isn't difficult if the judgment creditor has some and you know where it is. But what do you do when you know only that the money exists, but have no idea how to find it? For example, you may know that a person works, but not where, or that he has money in the bank, but not which one. Wouldn't it be nice to simply ask the judgment debtor a few questions which he had to answer?

Well, thanks to California Code of Civil Procedure Section 117.19(b), you can do just that. Here's how it works. When a Small Claims Court judgment is entered against a person (or business) the loser must fill out a form entitled the "Judgment Debtor's Statement of Assets." This form must be sent to the person who won the case within 35 days after Notice of Entry of Judgment is mailed out by the clerk unless the loser pays off the judgment, appeals or makes a motion to vacate the judgment. If the defendant appeals or files a motion to vacate and subsequently loses, he or she has 30 days to pay or fill out the Judgment Debtor's Statement.

C. Recovering Collection Costs And Interest

Costs incurred prior to recovering a judgment should be included in the judgment total. I discuss this in Chapter 15 C.

Here I am concerned with costs incurred after judgment. These are the costs that result when the judgment debtor doesn't pay voluntarily and you have had to levy on his or her assets. This can be expensive and you will want to make the judgment debtor pay, if possible. Many costs of collecting a judgment are recoverable, some are not. Generally speaking, you can recover your direct costs of collecting which include such things as sheriff fees, fees to get papers (i.e., "Writ of Execution," "Abstract of Judgment") issued, and recording fees. You can also recover interest on the judgment at a rate of 10% per year. Indirect costs such as babysitting costs, time off from work, postage, gasoline, etc., can't be recovered.

There are two principal ways to collect your costs:

1. Writ Of Execution

If you will turn back a few pages to the sample "Writ of Execution" you will see that as part of levying on wages, bank accounts, automobiles, businesses, etc., collection fees can simply be added to the total to be collected. These include the fee for issuing the Writ of Execution and the sheriff's fee for collecting it. This can really add up as the sheriff's fees for selling a motor vehicle, or placing a keeper at a place of business are considerable. In addition, you can collect any interest that has accrued on the original judgment.

2. Memorandum Of Credits, Accrued Interest And Costs After Judgment

Other costs, such as money expended for an "Abstract of Judgment," County Recorder fees and costs for unsuccessful levies on wages, bank accounts, businesses or motor vehicles can be recovered only after court approval. To get these you must file a "Memorandum of Credits, Accrued Interest and Costs After Judgment." The Small Claims Court clerk will help you prepare this form. File one copy with the clerk and have a friend mail another copy to the judgment debtor. Then have your friend fill out a "Proof of Service" (see Chapter 11 F) to be filed with the clerk.

WARNING! Judgment debtors who don't fill out the form may be held in contempt of court which means that a fine or, in theory, even a sentence of a few days in jail could be imposed.

WINNER'S NOTE: If you won your Small Claims Court case, have not been paid and no appeal has been filed, you are entitled to receive the Judgment Debtor's Statement of Assets form. If you don't receive this form within 35 days from the day the clerk mails you the notice that you won the case or if you do get the form and the judgment debtor hasn't filled it out in good faith, see the Small Claims Court clerk and ask that procedures be instituted to require that the judgment debtor appear before a judge.[10]

NAME AND ADDRESS OF ATTORNEY:	TELEPHONE:	FOR COURT USE ONLY:
Peter Plaintiff 123 Broadway Albany, CA ATTORNEY FOR IN PRO PER	848-7938	

Name of court, branch, judicial district, mailing and street address:

PLAINTIFF:
Peter Plaintiff

DEFENDANT:
Doris Defendant

MEMORANDUM OF CREDITS, ACCRUED INTEREST AND COSTS AFTER JUDGMENT	CASE NUMBER:

MEMORANDUM OF CREDITS

CREDIT for payments and partial satisfaction of judgment, including direct payments and executions partially satisfied:

$_____
(if none, state none)

INTEREST ACCRUED AFTER JUDGMENT

INTEREST ACCRUED AFTER JUDGMENT at 7% from date of entry of judgment on balance due after dates of payments or credits acknowledged above: $_____

MEMORANDUM OF COSTS AFTER JUDGMENT

1 Costs after judgment claimed on memorandum filed heretofore: . . . . $_____
2 Clerk's fees: . . . . $_____
3 _____ $_____
4 Sheriff's, marshal's or constable's fees: . . . . $_____
5 _____ $_____
6 Serving supplementary proceedings: . . . . $_____
7 _____ $_____
8 Notary fees: . . . . $_____
9 _____ $_____
10 _____ $_____
TOTAL $_____

Executed on _____ at _____, California.
        (Date)   (Place)

_____
(Signature of Declarant)

_____
(Type or Print Name of Declarant)

NOTE: A notice of motion to tax costs shall specify the items of the cost bill to which objection is made.
(See reverse side for Declaration of Service and Acknowledgment of Service)

MEMORANDUM OF CREDITS, ACCRUED INTEREST
AND COSTS AFTER JUDGMENT   C.C.P. Secs. 682.2, 1033.7, 2015.5

---

[10] This proceeding is called an "Order for Appearance of the Judgment Debtor." You may ask the "judgment debtor" to give you the information asked for on the form. If s/he refuses, ask the judge to find him/her in contempt of court. If s/he fails to show, the judge will issue a warrant for that person's arrest.

25.

Where Do We Go
From Here?

It's easy to criticize the existing legal system--almost everyone knows that it's on the rocks. The $350 a day experts with their degrees, titles, and well-funded consulting companies have studied the problem to death with no positive results. And this is hardly surprising, since most of the experts involved in the studies and in the resulting decisions are lawyers who, at bottom, are unable to understand a problem of which they are so thoroughly a part.[1]

---

[1] Not everyone believes that a rotten court system is a bad thing. David Hapgood, in his interesting book, The Average Man Fights Back, reports the following statement by the Chinese Emperor K'ang Hsi: "...lawsuits would tend to increase to a frightening extent if people were not afraid of the tribunals and if they felt confident of always finding in them ready and perfect justice...I desire therefore that those who have recourse to the tribunals should be treated without pity and in such a manner that they shall be disgusted with law and tremble to appear before a magistrate."

But instead of my lecturing you about all the things that are wrong at the local courthouse, let's sit down at the kitchen table with a pot of tea and a bowl of raspberries and see if we can't design a better system. After all, this republic was founded by ordinary people taking the law into their own hands--they had to because most of the governor, judge and lawyer-types were quite comfortable in England, thank you. And don't forget that we have already agreed that the present legal structure doesn't work, so we obviously have nothing to lose by making our own suggestions. Hey, leave a few raspberries for me, and why don't you jot down a few of your own ideas as we go along so that this becomes a two-way communication.

Before we get to specific suggestions for change, let's take a brief look around to see where we are starting from. As a society, we obviously have a fixation with trying to solve problems by suing one another. Nowhere in the world do people come close to being as litigious as we do. The result of this love of lawsuits, or perhaps its cause--it's one of those chicken and egg problems--is the fact that, whenever we get into any sort of spat with anyone, or even think that we might get into one in the future, we run to a lawyer.[2] It's gotten so bad that people who suffer an injury have been known to call their lawyer before their doctor. But there is an odd paradox here. At the same time that we tolerate vast numbers of lawyers eating at the top end of our societal trough and are more and more likely to use them, public opinion polls tell us that our respect for lawyers has fallen so that we rate their trustworthiness below that of used car salespeople, undertakers and loan sharks. It's as if, the less we respect lawyers, the more we use them. Perhaps we're afraid that if we don't sue first, someone will get the jump on us. If you eat one more of those raspberries, I'll see you in court.

---

2 There are close to six hundred thousand lawyers in the United States, and another 120,000 in law schoool. New York City alone has more than 40,000. There are more judges in Los Angeles County than there are in all of France.

Have you ever thought about how people solved their disputes in other ages? Let's pretend for a moment that we are members of a society of deer hunters in an age when such things were still possible.[3] One fine fall morning we both set out bow in hand, you to the east and I to the west. Before long, you hit a high cliff and turn north. My way is blocked by a swift river, and I too turn north. Without our realizing it, our paths converge. Suddenly, a great stag jumps from the underbrush and we both pull back our bows and let fly. Our arrows pierce the deer's heart from opposite sides, seemingly at the same instant.

For a moment we stand frozen, each surprised by the presence of the other. Then we realize what has happened and that we have a problem. To whom does the deer belong? We carry the deer back to the village, each unwilling to surrender our claim to the other. After the deer is gutted and hung, we go to speak to the chief of our group who convenes a council of elders to meet late in the afternoon. Each of us has his say as to what happened. The deer carcass is examined. Anyone else who has knowledge of our dispute is invited to speak. Tribal customs (laws) are consulted, our credibility is weighed, and a decision is made--in time for dinner.

Now, let's ask ourselves what would happen today, if you and I simultaneously shot a deer (instead of each other) on the first day of hunting season and were unable to agree to whom it belonged. Assuming we didn't fight it out on the spot, but wanted the dispute resolved by "proper" legal procedures, lawyers would have to be consulted, court papers filed and responded to, a court appearance scheduled, words spoken in legalese, and a formal court decision written and issued. All of this for a deer that would have long since rotted away unless it had been put in cold storage. If the deer had been frozen, the storage costs would have to be added to court costs and attorney fees which all together would surely add up to a lot more than the value of the deer. Oh well, next time we had better go

---

3 Anthropologists will, I hope, accept this little fable as just that.

hunting at McDonald's where everything is delivered safely in plastic.

Seriously, what were the differences between the ways that the two societies resolved the problem of who owned the deer? The so-called primitive one did a better job, but why? Obviously because their solution was in proportion to the problem, while today we make the solution process so cumbersome and expensive that it dwarfs most disputes. The hunting society handled the disagreement quickly, cheaply and, most importantly, with a process that allowed the disputing parties to participate in and understand what was going on.[4] Simple, you say. Why then can't our dispute resolution procedure achieve even one of these goals? In large measure, because lawyers have vested financial and psychic interests in the present cumbersome way of doing things and have neither the motivation nor the perspective to make changes.

But isn't my view a bit radical? Isn't there something uniquely valuable about the great sweep of the common law down through the ages? Doesn't the majestic black-robed judge sitting on his throne mumbling esoteric nonsense somehow guarantee that God is in heaven, the republic safe, and that "justice will be done?" Not necessarily. History is arbitrary--our dispute resolution mechanisms could have developed in a number of ways. If our present system worked well, imposing it on the future would make sense. As, in fact, it hardly works at all, continuing it is silly. Those who get quite misty-eyed recounting the history, traditions and time-tested forms behind our present ways of doing things are almost always people who benefit by their continuance. Consider, too, that in North America we have no pure legal tradition, having borrowed large hunks of our jurisprudence from England, Spain, France, Holland, and Germany, as well as various Native American cultures.

---

4 In a criminal case (if one hunter had attacked and injured the other) you would also want to think about restitution (making whole) to the injured person and perhaps to his dependents.

O.K., granted that there have been legal systems that worked better than ours, and granted that at least some change is overdue, what should we do? One significant reform would be to expand Small Claims Court. Like the system followed by the deer hunters, but unlike most aspects of our legal system, Small Claims Court is simple, fast, cheap and allows for the direct participation of the disputing parties. Never mind that up to now Small Claims Court has been tolerated as a way to keep lawyer's offices clear of penny ante people with penny ante disputes. It's there, it works, and we can expand it to play a meaningful role in our lives.

As you know by now, Small Claims Court as it is presently set up has several disadvantages. First, the amount that can be sued for is ridiculously low. Second, the court only has the power to make judgments that can be satisfied by the payment of money damages. Third, many kinds of cases, such as divorces, adoptions, etc., aren't permitted. Why not start our effort to improve things by doing away with these disadvantages? Let's raise the maximum amount that can be sued for to $10,000.[5] I would like to suggest $20,000, but perhaps we should take one step at a time to limit attorney opposition. An increase to $10,000 would be a significant reform--allowing tens of thousands of disputes to be removed from our formal legal system. One logical reason to pick $10,000 is that people can't afford lawyers to handle disputes for amounts below this.[6] To illustrate, let's take a situation where Randy the carpenter agrees to do $20,000 worth of rehabilitation to Al's home. When the work is completed, an argument

■-■-■-■-■ ★❶★ ■-■-■-■-■

---

5 While most states limit Small Claims jurisdiction to the $1,000-$1,500 range, there are exceptions. For example, the United States Tax Court has a very successful Small Claims procedure which allows claims up to $10,000.

6 I believe that there are persuasive reasons for limiting the role of lawyers in addition to the fact that they cost too much. Such a limitation would require fundamental changes in our adversary system and is the subject for a broader book. For a good history of how our adversary system evolved from barbaric practices such as trial by battle, how it all too often serves to obscure rather than expose the truth, and how it protects the interests of the already strong and powerful (those who can afford a good mouthpiece) at the expense of everyone else, see Injustice For All, Strick, Putnam, $8.95.

develops about whether the work was done properly according to the agreement. Al pays Randy $15,000, leaving $5,000 in dispute. Randy goes to his lawyer, and Al to his. Each has several preliminary conferences after which the lawyers exchange several letters and telephone calls. Eventually, a lawsuit is filed and answered, a court date is obtained many months in the future and then changed several times, and, finally, a two-hour trial is held. Randy's lawyer bills him $1,255 (25 hours x $50 per hour) and Al's charges $960 (24 hours x $40 per hour), for a total fee of $2,215. The dispute takes eleven months to be decided. In the end, Randy is awarded $3,500 of the $5,000.

This is a typical case with a typical solution. Between them, the lawyers collected almost half of the amount in dispute and took most of a year to arrive at a solution that very likely left both Randy and Al frustrated. Don't you think that Randy and Al would have preferred presenting their case in Small Claims Court where it would have been heard and decided in a month? Of course, either of them could have done worse arguing the case himself, but remember, when the legal fees are taken into consideration, the loser would have had to do a lot worse before he was out-of-pocket any money. Randy recovered $3,500 with a lawyer, but after subtracting the $1,255 lawyer fee, his net gain was only $2,245. Al ended up paying $4,460 ($3,500 for the judgment and $960 for his attorney). Thus, if a Small Claims Court judge had awarded Randy any amount from $2,246 to $4,459, both men would have done better than they did with lawyers. Of course, if this sort of case were permitted in Small Claims Court, there would be two big losers. Can it be a coincidence that lawyers (through their influence in state legislatures) make sure that Small Claims maximums are kept as low as possible?

The second great barrier to bringing cases in Small Claims Court is the fact that, with a minor exception, the court is limited to make money judgments. Think back for a moment to our problems with the twice-shot deer. How does the award of money make sense in this situation? In our Small Claims

Court, the Indian who didn't end up with the carcass
would have had to sue the other for the fair market
value of the deer. What nonsense--if we are going to
have a dispute resolution procedure, why not permit a
broad range of solutions such as the deer being cut in
half, or the deer going to one hunter and six ducks
going to the other in compensation, or maybe even the
deer going to the person who needed it most. Using
an example more common at the end of the 20th cen-
tury, why not allow a Small Claims Court judge to
order an apartment be cleaned, a garage repainted, or
a car properly fixed, instead of simply telling one
person to pay X dollars to the other. One advantage
of this sort of flexibility is that more judgments
would be meaningful. Under our present system, tens
of thousands of judgments can't be collected because
the loser has no obvious source of income. We need
to get away from the notion that people who are broke
have neither rights nor responsibilities. All people
need both.

Lawyers and judges often contend that it would
be impossible to enforce judgments granted under a
more flexible approach. Perhaps some would be hard
to keep track of. Certainly it might require some
experimentation to find out what types of judgments
will work and which will not; however, since it is
often impossible to collect a judgment under the
present system, it can't hurt to try some alternatives.

The third big change that I propose, and the one
that would truly make over our court system, involves
expanding the types of cases that can be heard in
Small Claims. Why not be brave and take the 20 most
common legal problems and adopt simplified procedures
enabling all of them to be handled by the people
themselves without lawyers? Why not open up our
courthouses to the average person who, after all,
pays the bills?

To accomplish this democratization of our dispute resolution procedures, I suggest dividing Small
Claims Court into several separate divisions, each one
responsible for a broad area of common concern. For
example, there would be a landlord-tenant and a

domestic relations division.[7] Each would have the
authority to consider a broad range of problems and
solutions falling within its area of concern. Today,
if you have a claim against your landlord (or he
against you) for money damages, you can use Small
Claims only if the claim is for $1,500 or less. If
you want a roof fixed, a tenant evicted, or to protect your privacy, etc., Small Claims Court can't
help you.[8] The Canadian province of British Columbia
has already put all landlord-tenant disputes in what
amounts to a Small Claims format, easily and cheaply
available to both landlord and tenant. Why can't we?

A domestic relations Small Claims Court could
include simplified procedures to help people handle
their own uncontested divorces, adoptions, name
changes, guardianships, etc. safely and cheaply. And
why not? Even with considerable hostility from lawyers and court personnel, over 20% of the divorces in
California are already handled without a lawyer.
When I suggest that people should be encouraged to
handle their own domestic problems in a Small Claims
type forum, I'm not advocating sensible safeguards be
dropped. For example, if a divorce involves children, you would want to have someone trained in the
field carefully examine the parents' plans for custody, visitation and support to see if they are reasonable.

Without going into detail, I suggest that if we
took lawyers out of our domestic relations courts, we
would save not only millions of dollars and hours,
but more importantly, we would lighten the heavy
burden of hostility and anxiety that the parties must
now bear. Our present system, in which parents and
children become clients to a "hired gun" (the lawyer)
is a bad one. By definition, the client role is weak
and the gun fighter role strong. This imbalance
commonly results in lawyers making critical decisions, affecting the client's lives, sometimes obvi-

---

7 There is nothing new about the idea of dividing a court by subject
matter. This is already done in our formal trials courts and works
well.

8 As I pointed out in Chapter 20, some evictions can be brought in
Small Claims if a number of conditions are met, but it is commonly
unwise to do so.

ously, sometimes subtly. All too often these decisions benefit the lawyer and his bank balance to the
detriment of both the client's psyche and pocketbook.
The lawyer, after all, is paid more to fight, or at
least to pretend to fight, than to compromise. I
have seen dozens of situations where lawyers have
played on people's worst instincts (paranoia, greed,
ego, one-upmanship) to fan nasty, little disagreements into flaming battles. Perhaps mercifully, the
battles normally last only as long as the lawyers'
bills are paid.[9]

I could list a number of other areas of law that
could be converted to a Small Claims approach (auto
accidents, simple probates, perhaps even some criminal cases), but I am sure you get the point. We must
take control of the decision making processes that
affect our lives. We must make ourselves welcome in
our own courts and legislatures. We must stop
looking at ourselves as clients and start taking
responsibility for our own legal decisions.

Let's assume now that no matter what the obsta-
cles, we are going to expand drastically the role of
Small Claims Court. In the process of so doing, we
will need to make a number of changes in the way the
court now operates. It will be a good opportunity to
throw out a number of existing procedures that owe
more to history than to common sense. Here are a few
ideas:

1. Before people present their dispute for
resolution as part of a court proceeding, they should
be encouraged to talk it over among themselves. This
seems to be basic common sense, but a face-to-face
meeting to find out if a compromise is possible isn't
part of the present system. A meeting with someone
who has training as a mediator could occur at the
courthouse or, perhaps, at a less intimidating location in the community, as a regular part of every
case.

---

9 In an interesting article entitled "Valuable Deficiencies, A Service Economy Needs People In Need," in the Fall 1977 Co-Evolution
Quarterly, John McNight points out that "The Latin root of the word
'client' is a verb which translates 'to hear,' 'to obey.'"

2. Let's make our court one of truly easy access. This means holding weekend and evening sessions. This is being done now on a limited basis in our larger counties, but should be routinely available everywhere. When court is held at 9 A.M. on weekdays, it often costs more in lost job time for all the principals and witnesses to show up than the case is worth.

3. Let's get the judge out of his black robe and off of his throne. There is a part of all of us that loves the drama involved in seeing our magistrate sitting on high like the king of England, but I am convinced by my own brief experience as a "pro tem" judge that this is counter productive. We would have a lot less confrontation, and a lot more willingness to compromise if we got rid of some of the drama.

4. While we're making changes, let's make a big one--let's restrict the adversary system.10 It contributes a great deal to posturing and obfuscation and little to arriving at a dispute resolution process that everyone can live with. We must move toward systems of mediation and arbitration in which, instead of a traditional judge, we have someone whose role is to facilitate the parties arriving at their own solution--deciding it for them only if they arrive at a hopeless impasse. Big business, big labor, and increasingly even lawyers are coming to realize that arbitration and mediation are good ways to solve problems.11 What I have in mind is something like this: All the parties to the dispute would sit down at a table with the Small Claims employee (let's drop the word "judge"). This person would be trained for the job, but would not normally be a lawyer. The court employee would help the par-

---

10 Roscoe Pound, distinguished legal scholar, said it better than I can: "The doctrine of contentious procedure...is peculiar to Anglo-American law...(it) disfigures our judicial administration at every point...(it) gives to the whole community a false notion of the purpose and end of law....Thus, the courts...are made agents or abettors of lawlessness." This quote is reported by Anne Strick in Injustice For All.

11 California has adopted an arbitration procedure which even allows cases that have been filed in court to be diverted to an arbitration procedure.

ties search for areas of agreement and possible compromise and then help them define any areas still in dispute.

5. Appeal rules should also be changed. The present California system which allows only the defendant to appeal to Superior Court and allows lawyers on appeals is nuts. All too often corporate defendants who have lawyers on retainer use the present system to frustrate consumers who have won in Small Claims Court. It is my belief that no appeals should be allowed in Small Claims Court--the amounts in question just aren't worth it. If appeals are allowed, lawyers should be prohibited.[12]

I don't mean to suggest that the changes I propose in this short chapter are the only ones necessary. If we are going to put the majority of our routine legal work in Small Claims, it will require turning our dispute resolution process on its head. Legal information must be stored and decoded so that it is available to the average person. Clerk's offices, and the other support systems surrounding our courts must be expanded and geared to serve the non-lawyer. Legal forms must be translated from "legalese" into English. Computer systems must be developed to bring information into our living rooms.

Let's illustrate how things might change by looking at a case I recently saw argued in a northern California Small Claims Court. One party to the dispute (let's call her Sally) arranged fishing charters for business and club groups. The other (let's call him Ben) owned several fishing boats. Sally often hired Ben's boats for her charters. Their relationship was of long standing and had been profitable to both. However, as the fishing charter business grew, both Sally and Ben began to enlarge their operations. Sally got a boat or two of her own and Ben began getting into the charter booking business. Eventually they stepped on one another's toes

---

12 Because of the so-called constitutional right to be represented by a lawyer if you want one, there will be problems eliminating both defendants' rights to appeal (or transfer) to a court where they can have a lawyer. One way to solve this dilemma is to set a Small Claims procedure that is so desirable that very few defendants will want their cases heard in a formal court.

and their friendy relationship was replaced by ten-
sion and arguments. One day a blow-up occurred over
some inconsequential detail, phones were slammed down
and Sally and Ben each swore never to do business
with the other again.

Before the day of the final fight, Sally had
organized two charters on Ben's boat. These were to
have taken place a week after the phones were slammed
down. For reasons unconnected with the argument, the
charters were cancelled by the clubs that had organized them. Ben had about a week's notice of cancel-
lation. He also had $600 in deposits that Sally had
paid him. He refused to refund the deposits. Sally
sued him in Small Claims Court for $700 ($600 for the
charter fee and $100 for general inconvenience).13

Testimony in court made it clear that charters
were commonly cancelled and were often replaced by
others booked at the last minute. Ben and Sally had
signed a "Standard Marine Charter Agreement" because
it was required by the Coast Guard, although they had
never in the past paid attention to its terms. They
had always worked out sensible adjustments on a
situation-by-situation basis, depending on whether
substitute charters were available and whether the
club or business cancelling had paid money up front,
etc.

When Ben and Sally first presented their arguments about the $700, it seemed that they were not
too far apart as to what would be a fair compromise.
Unfortunately, the adversary nature of the court
system encouraged each to overstate his (her) case
and to dredge up all sorts of irrelevant side issues.
"What about the times you overloaded my boat?" Ben
demanded. "How about those holidays when you price
gouged me?" Sally replied. As the arguments went
back and forth, each person got angrier and angrier
and was less and less able to listen to the other.

The result was that after an hour of testimony
the judge was left with a confused mish-mash of cus-
tom, habit, maritime charter contracts, promises made

---

13 As we learned earlier, Sally can't recover for inconvenience, so
her maximum recovery would be $600.

or not made, past performance, etc. No decision that
he arrived at was likely to be accepted by both Ben
and Sally as being fair. Indeed, unless he gave one
or the other everything he or she requested, both of
them would surely feel cheated. That is not to say
that the hearing was all bad--some good things did
occur. The dispute was presented quickly, cheaply
and each person got to have his or her say and blow
off some steam. All of these things would have been
impossible in our formal court system. However, if
Small Claims Court could be changed along the lines
suggested above, a better result might have been
reached.

Suppose that instead of a formal courtroom
approach Ben and Sally are first encouraged to sit
down and talk the dispute out. If this fails, then
the next step is to sit down in a non-courtroom
setting with a court employee who is trained as a
mediator and whose purpose is to help Ben and Sally
arrive at a fair compromise--a compromise which might
provide a foundation for Ben and Sally to continue to
work together in the future. Only if compromise is
impossible, would there be recourse to more formal
proceedings.14 I am convinced that Ben and Sally
would have worked out a compromise at the first or
second stage.

One final point. Today lawyers are still trying
to plug the holes in the rotten dike of our present
legal system. Tomorrow the dike will burst and many
of our present ways of doing things will be washed
into the history books. Small Claims Court will
survive the deluge and will expand. The danger is
that lawyers will try to control Small Claims Court
so that their attitudes and prejudices dominate it as
they have dominated every other mechanism our society
has to resolve disputes. To allow this to happen is
to destroy much of the value of expanding Small
Claims Courts. And don't minimize the danger. As I
have noted, under a so-called "consumer reform"

---

14 If we put domestic cases into Small Claims Court (and even if we
don't), it is essential that we work out a non-adversary way of
handling them so that bitterness and bad feelings are kept to a minimum instead of inflated as is now the case.

approach, lawyers are already serving in the role of
Small Claims advisor. It is all too likely that
under the guise of trying to protect us from ourselves, an effort will also be made to have everyone
see a lawyer as part of the Small Claims procedure.
Remember, it is our lawyer-dominated state legislature that makes Small Claims rules and our lawyer-
dominated Judicial Council that carries them out.

About the Author

Ralph is the leader of the "do your own law" movement on the West Coast. As a co-founder of Nolo Press and the author of numerous books and articles aimed at giving the non-lawyers "legal information" to deal with their own life decisions, he has constantly tried to expand the areas in which people can help themselves.

Ralph has a license to practice law. He doesn't use it. Instead he gives lectures and workshops on such subjects as "Tenant's Rights," "Law For Unmarried Couples," "How To Use Small Claims Court," "Debt Problems," etc. to groups all over California. As part of doing research for this book, Ralph has served as a Small Claims Court judge (pro tem) in Berkeley, California.

Ralph, along with Toni Ihara, is the author of 29 Reasons Not to Go to Law School.

Index

self-help law books

BUSINESS & FINANCE

HOW TO FORM YOUR OWN CALIFORNIA CORPORATION
All the forms, Bylaws, Articles, stock cer-
tificates and instructions necessary to file
your small profit corporation in California.
Calif. Edition $21.95

THE NON-PROFIT CORPORATION HANDBOOK: Includes all the forms, Bylaws, Articles &
instructions you need to form a non-profit
corporation in California.
Calif. Edition $19.95

BANKRUPTCY: DO IT YOURSELF: Step-by-step
instructions and all the forms you need.
National edition $12.95

LEGAL CARE FOR YOUR SOFTWARE: Protect your
software through the use of trade secret,
tradework, copyright, patent and contractual
laws and agreements. National Ed. $19.95

THE PARTNERSHIP BOOK: A basic primer for
people who are starting a small business
together. Sample agreements, buy-out
clauses, limited partnerships. $15.95

PLAN YOUR ESTATE: WILLS, PROBATE AVOIDANCE,
TRUSTS & TAXES: Making a will, alternatives
to probate, limiting inheritance & estate
taxes, living trusts, etc. $15.95

CHAPTER 13: THE FEDERAL PLAN TO REPAY YOUR
DEBTS: The alternative to straight bankruptcy. This book helps you develop a plan
to pay your debts over a 3 year period.
All forms & worksheets included. $12.95

BILLPAYERS' RIGHTS: Bankruptcy, student
loans, bill collectors & collection agencies, credit cards, car repossessions,
child support, etc. $9.95

THE CALIFORNIA PROFESSIONAL CORPORATION
HANDBOOK: All the forms & instructions
to form a professional corporation. $19.95

SMALL TIME OPERATOR: How to start &
operate your own small business, keep
books, pay taxes. $8.95

WE OWN IT!: Legal, tax & management
information you need to operate co-ops
& collectives. $9.00

FAMILY & FRIENDS

HOW TO DO YOUR OWN DIVORCE: All the
forms for an uncontested dissolution.
Calif. Edition $9.95

CALIFORNIA MARRIAGE & DIVORCE LAW:
Community & separate property, debts,
children, buying a house, etc. Sample
marriage contracts, simple will, probate avoidance information. $12.95

AFTER THE DIVORCE: HOW TO MODIFY
ALIMONY, CHILD SUPPORT & CHILD CUSTODY:
How to increase alimony or child support, decrease what you pay, change custody & visitation, etc. $14.95

THE LIVING TOGETHER KIT: Legal guide
for unmarried couples. Sample will &
living together contract. $8.95

SOURCEBOOK FOR OLDER AMERICANS: Most
comprehensive resource tool on income,
rights & benefits of Americans over 55.
Social security, Medicare, etc. $10.95

HOW TO ADOPT YOUR STEPCHILD: How to
prepare all forms & appear in court.
                                $14.95

A LEGAL GUIDE FOR LESBIAN/GAY COUPLES:
Raising children, buying property, wills,
etc. $12.95

RULES & TOOLS

THE PEOPLE'S LAW REVIEW: A compendium of
people's law resources. 50-state catalog
of self-help law materials; articles &
interviews. $8.95

FIGHT YOUR TICKET! Radar, drunk driving,
preparing for court, arguing your case,
cross-examining witnesses, etc. $12.95

LEGAL RESEARCH: HOW TO FIND AND UNDERSTAND
THE LAW: Comprehensive guide to doing
your own legal research. $12.95

CALIFORNIA TENANTS' HANDBOOK: Everything
tenants need to know to protect themselves. $9.95

EVERYBODY'S GUIDE TO SMALL CLAIMS COURT:
Step-by-step guide to going to small
claims court. $9.95

HOW TO CHANGE YOUR NAME: All the forms &
instructions you need. $10.95

PROTECT YOUR HOME WITH A DECLARATION OF
HOMESTEAD: All the forms & instructions
to homestead your home. $8.95

MARIJUANA: YOUR LEGAL RIGHTS: All the
legal information users & growers need to
guarantee their constitutional rights &
protect their privacy. $9.95

AUTHOR LAW: Comprehensive explanation of
the legal rights of authors. $14.95

UNEMPLOYMENT BENEFITS HANDBOOK: Everything you need to know about your benefits. $5.95

LANDLORDING: Maintenance and repairs,
getting good tenants, avoid evictions,
taxes, etc. $15.00

DON'T SIT IN THE DRAFT: A comprehensive
draft counseling guide. $6.95

PACIFIC RIM SERIES

CALIFORNIA DREAMING: THE POLITICAL
ODYSSEY OF PAT AND JERRY BROWN: The
story of the First Family of California
Politics from the Gold Rush to the
1980s. $9.95

IN A LIGHTER VEIN . . .

29 REASONS NOT TO GO TO LAW SCHOOL: A
humorous and irreverent look at the
dubious pleasures of going to law school.
                                     $4.95

Order Form

QUANTITY	TITLE	UNIT PRICE	TOTAL

Prices subject to change

☐ Please send me a
   catalogue of your books

Tax: (California only) 6½% for Bart,
     Los Angeles, San Mateo & Santa
     Clara counties; 6% for all others

SUBTOTAL _____

Tax _____

Postage & Handling $1.00

TOTAL _____

Name _____

Address _____

_____

Send to:

NOLO PRESS
950 Parker St.
Berkeley, CA 94710
       or
NOLO DISTRIBUTING
Box 544
Occidental, CA 95465